CRAFTING THE

MOSAIC

CELEBRATING 75 YEARS
OF CRAFT IN MANITOBA

© Manitoba Crafts Museum and Library, 2007

1B-183 Kennedy Street
Winnipeg, Manitoba, Canada
R3C 1S6

Printed in Canada on acid-free paper by Friesens.

Book and cover design by Doowah Design Inc.
Photography by Robert Barrow

Library and Archives Canada Cataloguing in Publication

Crafting the mosaic : celebrating 75 years of craft in Manitoba.

Includes bibliographical references.

ISBN 978-0-9730586-1-1

1. Handicraft--Manitoba--Catalogs.
2. Material culture--Manitoba--Catalogs.
3. Manitoba Crafts Museum and Library--Catalogs. I. Manitoba Crafts Museum and Library

TT6.C32W56 2007   745.5097127   C2007-901530-1

The Manitoba Crafts Museum and Library gratefully acknowledges the financial assistance of The Winnipeg Foundation, the Department of Culture, Heritage and Tourism (Heritage Grants Program), and Young Canada Works.

ACKNOWLEDGEMENTS

Although this publication has been truly a group effort, with many volunteers assisting with planning, background work, research, writing, decision making and collections work, there are many individuals who must be thanked by name.

The initial shortlist of some 200 artifacts was compiled by Dot From, June Cameron, Gerdine Strong, Susanne Sulkers, and Risé Thompson.

The Selection Committee who whittled down the initial selection of artifacts to about 85 pieces included Stephanie Cooper, Carol James, Carol Kaye, Alan Lacovetsky and Edward Tabachek.

The research was done in part by Daniela Smith-Fernandez during the summer of 2006, and a final selection of 75 pieces was made after this stage of the project.

Many individuals were consulted during the research stage including:

Martha Black, Curator of Aboriginal Art, Royal British Colombia Museum; Sarah Beam, Assistant curator, Bata Shoe Museum; Persis Clarkson, Faculty of Anthropology, University of Winnipeg; Stephanie Cooper, Hudson's Bay Company Collection, Manitoba Museum; Stan Freer, Faculty of Anthropology, University of Manitoba; Manju Lodha; Wendy Molnar; Natalia Nekrassova, Curator, Textile Museum of Canada; Katherine Pettipas, Curator of Aboriginal Art, Manitoba Museum; Barbara-Anne Ramer, Ontario Handweavers and Spinners, Master Spinner; Gloria Romaniuk, Oseredok Ukrainian Cultural and Educational Center Archives; Carol Romanyk, Ukrainian Museum of Manitoba; Mary-Anne Steggles, Asian Art Department, University of Manitoba; Jo-Anne Tabachek; Christine Tabbernor, Ogniwo Polish Museum Society Inc; Orysia Tracz, Lynn Valde, Northern Images; Darlene Coward Wight, Curator of Inuit Art, Winnipeg Art Gallery; Robin K. Wright, Curator of Native American Art, Burke Museum;

Translation assistance was received from Laverne Carlson and Karen Jacks.

The text for the artifacts was written in large part by Curator Andrea Reichert, with volunteers Julia Broderick (37,70), Dot From (4, 5, 21, 23, 29, 46, 48, 50, 53, 64, 69), Carol James (72), Carol Kaye (6, 11, 20, 27, 45) and Brigitte de March (44) writing text for specific pieces.

Proofing was assisted by Paul D. Earl, Dot From, Carol Kaye, Ernie Reichert and Ginny Toni.

The foreword was prepared by Patricia Bovey.

The book was designed by Doowah Design Inc.

Assistance from Friesens was greatly appreciated.

FOREWORD
CRAFT: INEXTRICABLE CONNECTIONS

**"the real value of craft – value in
a contemporary holistic sense"**

– Michele Hardy, 'Crafts and Knowledge' 1994

Much has been written about the crafts over the years, its materials, the 'making' of objects and the backgrounds of the generations of craftspeople, from many cultures, who have created magnificent, useful and meaningful objects over many centuries. Handcrafts from past civilizations have taught us about their respective societies, the ways of life, values, their aesthetic principles and available materials. With this anniversary volume we are celebrating the crafts and craftspeople of Manitoba and the visually rich and diverse traditions of this place.

The word 'craft', originally meaning 'cunning power', is now defined as 'skill, strength and intelligence' and the 'craftsperson' is described as requiring specific knowledge and ability to create their objects. At the grassroots of human creativity, the crafts have often been the work of anonymous makers, and at times works and craftspeople have assumed a place among the work of major international artists of all media. The maxim of one 20th century Japanese weaving workshop is *"to construct the present based on tradition"*, or *"crafting our present from the heart of tradition"* [1]. This is equally true for Manitoba's craft community. The crafts inextricably link the present to the past, and at once connect the maker, the viewer, the user, the environment in which the piece was made and the society it reflects. Crafts create connections for future generations as they come to understand the place of personal creativity in past times.

Particular objects have always been necessities for daily living, both in domestic and religious settings including clothes, pots, tools, dishes and cooking and eating utensils. In pre-industrial times these objects had to be hand-made. Some of the functional crafted items were basic in form and decoration; others quite beautiful and sophisticated. As with crafts world-wide, many of the 'one of a kind' objects in the collection of the Manitoba Crafts Museum and Library were created to be used, and appreciated, in the course of daily life. They were made to meet basic human needs, the knitted and woven woolen garments for protection against the weather; wooden and clay bowls and pots for cooking and eating; embroidered shirts and blouses for special occasions; baby clothes and blankets; and jewelry and other personal ornaments. Objects were also created for spiritual and ritual use, the crosses, Menorahs, communion cups, and more. All of these pieces are personal to the owner or the community of owners or users.

At times crafts are made by groups of individuals working together. This is true, for instance, in the strong Manitoba craft of quilting, the quilters meeting regularly and creating their work together in a community. These works then become as much about the relationships of the makers with each other and with the quilt, as they do with the object, made to give warmth and comfort in its visual symphony of shapes, patterns and colours. Crafts are hand-made, not mass-made objects, and thus always remain linked to the hand of the maker.

In our post-industrial, high tech age, the necessary objects for daily living are mass-made and mass-marketed. With such easy access to our domestic basic necessities, the place of the unique hand-crafted works has changed in our personal world and they take on new meanings in our lives. Hand created objects now tend

---

[1] Millie R. Creighton, *"Nostalgia, Gender and Identity: Woven in 100 Per Cent Silk"*, *Making and Metaphor: A Discussion of Meaning in Contemporary Craft, Canadian Museum of Civilization*, p. 101, 1994

to be the 'more special' things in our homes and are not 'used', perhaps, to the degree they had been in earlier times. They are often 'on display' as our own 'treasured items'. Simultaneously, the work of contemporary craft artists is now sought after by collectors, and art galleries and museums have presented many major exhibitions of craft work. Some of the craft artists represented in the collection of the MANITOBA CRAFTS MUSEUM AND LIBRARY are among those who have been featured in public exhibitions and publications. Such work is considered both craft and art– craft because of roots and function; art because of the experimentation with new ideas, the uniqueness of expression and the resulting quality achieved in each piece.

The craftsperson of every era has had a particular sensitivity to, and feeling for, their materials and their properties. The lines or fissures in a piece of soapstone, for instance, often gave Inuit artists the inspiration for the form a sculpture would take, and the knots and veining in a piece of wood are creatively incorporated into a bowl or other object. Likewise, the knowledge of particular clays, glazes and firing temperatures; the understanding of the malleability of various metals; the making of dyes from plants and materials of the region; or the various textures of threads and wools in the weaving and embroidery of fabrics, are all critical to the success of making crafts. In developing the important elements of form, function and decoration, the craftsperson creates works in which the colours, shape, lines and feel is unique. The most skilled craft artists of every generation have also always found ways for personal expression in their work, and through time have extended the traditional boundaries of form, material and decoration. These developments have kept craft as a stimulating field of experimentation, engagement and one of real connection between the maker and the viewer or holder.

The collection of the MANITOBA CRAFTS MUSEUM AND LIBRARY is primarily of work from the post-industrial age. It traces the customs and creative expression of Aboriginal crafts and those of the diverse cultures who came to Manitoba, collectively making this province a truly rich oasis. The earliest works in the collection of the MUSEUM are relatively simple and plain, a spoon for example, fashioned out of wood and rather rudimentary in form and technique; toys, unassuming and practical; and the homespun fabrics for clothing of natural fibers. The later works add to the Manitoba mosaic. Through the collection one can see the richness and tradition of Ukrainian embroidery; detailed exquisite straw weavings, the changing styles and types of ceramics, the development of new means of working in glass, and the great varieties in weaving and fashion design. In addition the collection also includes some of the first Inuit carvings to come to the south in the 1950s and 1960s, many of them unsigned and identified only by the region from where they came.

Over the past 75 years, the dedication of the founders and volunteers of the MANITOBA CRAFT GUILD, and subsequently the MANITOBA CRAFTS MUSEUM AND LIBRARY, has been truly commendable. Their understanding of the significance of the crafts made in Manitoba was remarkable and their work has also done much to connect Manitoba's craftspeople, past and present, with audiences and collectors in the province and from elsewhere.

Traditional and contemporary crafts will continue to connect makers, viewers and users, inextricably, while also linking the past with the present. The craftspeople of Manitoba have produced truly significant work.

Patricia Bovey

INTRODUCTION

"Any irregularity or unevenness in the product is not always a manufacturing defect but an assurity that this is a genuine hand made product. It creates a beauty unmatched by any mass produced material"
— CRAFT RESOURCE CENTER, CALCUTTA, INDIA

The above was printed on a tag attached to a hand woven scarf that I recently received as a gift. After reading it, I pondered what a message like this really means. Is it a legal disclaimer of sorts releasing the craftsperson from any responsibility for imperfections in the final product and the retailer from having people return items due to defects? Is it a warning to the buyer that the item will not be *"perfectly manufactured"*, and that one should be wary of purchasing such an item? Or is it a *"charity case statement"*, written to make one feel good about purchasing something made in a developing country, despite any problems with the item? My sincere hope is that this type of tag is attached with pride by the craftsperson wishing to draw attention to the fact that the piece is hand made.

When the PERMANENT COLLECTION of the MANITOBA BRANCH OF THE CANADIAN HANDICRAFTS was established in 1933, the decline of hand made items was a major concern of the members. During the latter part of the 19th century, industrial manufacturing began to satisfy many areas of human need. Clothing, furniture, household items, transportation, food, and even art were available in a mass produced form. GUILD members sought to temper this trend with the creation of their collection of hand crafted items.

Another interest of early GUILD members was the increasing number of immigrants, mainly from Eastern Europe, that were arriving in Canada and were finding it difficult to fit into the community. In 1928, the New Canadian Folksong and Handicrafts Festival was held in the Canadian Pacific Railway's Royal Alexandra Hotel in Winnipeg. This successful festival was co-sponsored by the CPR and the CANADIAN HANDICRAFTS GUILD. Specifically, the festival organizers hoped to introduce new Canadians from countries such as Poland, the Ukraine, Italy, Germany, Romania, Sweden, Iceland and Russia to more established British Canadians. Crafts and the performing arts were recognized as media through which the various groups of people could communicate and appreciate each other's skills, talents and culture. Originally the Montreal Branch had planned to organize the event at a distance using a small local committee, but the prairie women being so independent, decided that they certainly didn't need Easterners to do that for them. Thus began the MANITOBA BRANCH OF THE CANADIAN HANDICRAFT GUILD[1].

The GUILD members also had a strong interest in improving the local community. To that end they assisted in the rural areas, particularly during the Great Depression, with workshops to help women make items for their families or to sell as an income supplement, often in partnership with the Women's Institutes. They also worked on rehabilitation of veterans returning from the battlefields of World War II and with children who had contracted polio. And, like many women's groups of the time, they assisted the Red Cross with war relief projects.

---

[1] The Canadian Handicrafts Guild – Manitoba Branch changed its name in the 1960s to the Crafts Guild of Manitoba. This name, or simply "The Guild", will be used to denote the organization from here on.

Of course, the CRAFTS GUILD OF MANITOBA was well known for the GUILD Shop where, for almost 70 years, Manitoba hand made items were sold to a wide variety of customers. For a long while it was the only shop in Winnipeg where hand made goods could be purchased and many items were purchased for prominent people, including Queen Elizabeth II and Pope John Paul II. Of course, many ordinary people also received wedding, baby and other gifts from the Shop. It is noteworthy that people still contact the MANITOBA CRAFTS MUSEUM AND LIBRARY to inquire about the Guild Shop, a full ten years since it closed - a testament to the impact that it had on the local community.

Throughout the history of the GUILD the members maintained a library collection. Initially developed to provide resource material for courses and workshops, the library has grown to include historical texts, *"how-to"* manuals, patterns, contemporary books, and general theory books on design and colour. The LIBRARY was named the GLADYS CHOWN MEMORIAL LIBRARY in 1948, after the president of the Guild who died quite suddenly while in office. The LIBRARY holdings number about 2,700 book titles and also include many journals, patterns, and vertical file materials.

The MANITOBA CRAFTS MUSEUM AND LIBRARY is grateful to Mrs. Stanislaw Zwolski, the wife of the Polish Consul to Winnipeg, who donated the first two artifacts to the Permanent Collection. Mrs. Zwolski had been involved with the GUILD, but her husband was called back to Poland in 1933. As a parting gift to the Guild she donated two dolls in traditional Polish costume.

From there the collection grew steadily. Members donated family heirlooms or items acquired while travelling abroad. Pieces were selected for the PERMANENT COLLECTION from merchandise initially intended for sale in the GUILD Shop, but deemed to be worthy of preservation. Other artifacts were acquired through projects initiated by GUILD members to mark anniversaries and other events. More recently, donations have come from members of the general public who share our goal of preserving and promoting craft. As of 2007, the collection numbers about 5,000 artifacts.

The collection itself reflects the nature of craft in Manitoba, particularly in the pre-1950 era. It consists of a wide variety of textile crafts including quilting, weaving, embroidery, lace, knitting, crochet, and batik, along with paper, wood, metal, glass, ceramic, and other non-textile media. It includes pieces from cultures around the world and from both men and women.

It was in the 1980s that the PERMANENT COLLECTION OF THE GUILD was transformed into a MUSEUM. The volunteers decided that the collection deserved to be exhibited more regularly, to be properly described and organized, and to be stored according to established museum standards. To this end, they attended workshops, sought advice of other museum professionals, and researched the best way to manage the museum. This work on the museum continued until the late 1990s, when the GUILD faced a series of new challenges.

The first challenge was the dissolution of the CRAFTS GUILD OF MANITOBA in 1997. After almost 70 years of operation, using volunteer labour almost exclusively, members decided that it was time to cease GUILD activities. It was a difficult decision that is still sometimes questioned today, but the GUILD Members chose to leave the Winnipeg community gracefully.

Pressures on the GUILD, including an ever-expanding variety of craft sellers, a diminishing supply of volunteer resources, and an increasing tax bill made this decision necessary. The question of what to do with the Museum and the Library collections then arose.

A decision taken by the CRAFTS GUILD OF MANITOBA BOARD to transfer the stewardship of the MUSEUM AND LIBRARY TO THE MANITOBA CRAFTS COUNCIL was to have long lasting ramifications. The COUNCIL, a contemporary craftsperson's organization, seemed like a good fit. The then named MANITOBA CRAFTS MUSEUM AND LIBRARY (MCML) would provide an historical anchor to their contemporary work. To help with the long-term upkeep of the Museum and Library, the GUILD established a fund at The Winnipeg Foundation using monies from the sale of their building and other assets. This fund, a key asset for the organization, initially totalled about $550,000 and continues to support MCML's activities.

A major event that occurred during the time spent in the care of the MANITOBA CRAFTS COUNCIL was a watermain break on June 8, 1999. In the middle of the night water poured into the space, eventually reaching a height of fifteen inches before a motion detector set off an alarm. This disaster damaged over 350 artifacts and a significant portion of the books. Overnight, the focus of the organization shifted from developing a new identity within the COUNCIL to basic survival. With 10-15% of the collection damaged by the water, MCML's public activities were completely halted. Over the next five years staff and volunteers worked to treat the artifacts, put the collection back in order and to re-establish a public presence. In 2001, the MANITOBA CRAFTS MUSEUM AND LIBRARY Committee made the difficult choice to separate from the MANITOBA CRAFTS COUNCIL.

By 2003 the independent MANITOBA CRAFTS MUSEUM AND LIBRARY was poised to open to the public once again and was moved downtown, coincidentally back into the old GUILD building on Kennedy Street. It seems a bit odd to say, but there appears to be a strong connection between the collections and this particular building. Since moving to the Kennedy Street location, staff and volunteers have been working to install exhibits, improve collections care, develop the library, offer programming and public events and increase the membership.

2007 marks the 75th year of the collections of the MANITOBA CRAFTS MUSEUM AND LIBRARY. This is quite an achievement for any museum collection in Manitoba, but more so considering all the challenges that this small museum has faced. It speaks volumes about the dedication of its volunteers and others involved with the organization.

Over the years as curator of the collection of the MANITOBA CRAFTS MUSEUM AND LIBRARY, I have made many observations about how the general public perceives craft. Specifically, it is interesting to hear the comments of visitors to the museum about the pieces in the collection. They often focus on time. Many ask, *"How long did it take to make this piece?"* Or they make the comment, *"I can't imagine how long it took to make that"*. This is often followed by, *"And they didn't have good lighting either"*. As a craftsperson of sorts myself, I find it interesting that this is often the first thing people ask me about my work. Perhaps it is a reflection of how busy our lives are now that most people simply cannot imagine spending any time making an item by hand.

Sometimes visitors comment on the skill of the craftsperson. Again, they cannot fathom how one would learn a technique like bobbin lace or glass blowing. Perhaps this is because, for many decades, most children have not grown up with craft in the home. Although there are exceptions, the daily practice of craft simply does not exist on a broad scale. Children do not learn these skills at their parents' or grandparents' knee anymore, something that the early Guild members foresaw and sought to prevent.

Finally, people seem to have a genuine connection to hand made items in general. There is a true fascination with things that have been made by other human beings. Sometimes this comes close to bewilderment about the time and energy to make the items, but there is always a respect that manufactured items do not receive. This is best illustrated by some of the donors who bring items to the MUSEUM for the collection. They often know nothing about the piece, but because it was made or owned by a grandmother, aunt, father or brother, they simply must find a good home for it.

We invite you to look through this book of 75 pieces that have been selected to represent the entire MANITOBA CRAFTS MUSEUM AND LIBRARY collection. The pieces are arranged in the order that they were acquired by the museum, which should provide a sense of the randomness of museum collection growth. It is truly impossible to predict who might walk through the door next to donate a fabulous item to the collection. We hope that you encounter a similar sense of surprise each time you turn a page.

Please take the time to truly look at the pieces. All crafts are an exercise in skill development, creative thinking, improvising, and sometimes sheer inspiration and problem-solving. Each craft, be it weaving, ceramics, or woodworking, involves the use of the hands, mind, heart and spirit of the craftsperson. All of the pieces that have been included in the book have been made by hand by real people across Manitoba, Canada and the world. Some were created as recently as a few years ago, while others were made as long as 1,000 years ago. Some pieces are completely functional and were intended to fulfill a basic need. Others are more decorative or celebratory and were meant to provide beauty and to nourish the creative soul of both the maker and the owner.

The multi-cultural and multi-faceted nature of our society has often been described as a mosaic - an image created by using small tiles or stones in a variety of colours. This word can also be used to describe the MCML collection, which has been developed through the acquisition of individual pieces that together form an entity that is worth more than the sum of its parts.

In conjunction with this book, the MANITOBA CRAFTS MUSEUM AND LIBRARY is hosting an exhibit of these artifacts in May 2007. The title of the exhibit is "MOSIAC", reflecting the many individual artifacts that make up the exhibit, and the varied nature of these pieces and their makers.

As a final note, each of the 75 pieces included here could have a tag attached to it warning of *"irregularity or unevenness"*. But it is these irregularities that make the pieces unique and connect us all though our shared humanness. Their beauty is enhanced, rather than diminished by these small variations in texture, colour and shape. Sophisticated machinery can produce millions of items exactly the same as each other, but these items will never achieve a place in the heart like those that are hand made. We hope that the treasures included in this book will find a place in your heart, as they have in ours.

Andrea Reichert
Curator, MANITOBA CRAFTS MUSEUM AND LIBRARY

CRAFTING THE

MOSAIC

CELEBRATING 75 YEARS
OF CRAFT IN MANITOBA

1. POLISH DOLLS

In 1933 Mrs. Stanislaw Zwolski, an experienced embroiderer and the wife of the Polish Consul in Winnipeg, donated the first two artifacts to the CRAFTS GUILD OF MANITOBA PERMANENT COLLECTION as a parting gift when her husband was called back to Poland. GUILD Members, who had always considered the establishment of a PERMANENT COLLECTION of historical craft an important part of the Guild mandate, were pleased with the donation, but were sad to see the President of the Polish Group at the GUILD leave.

The costumes worn by the dolls, which are cloth with straw and wool stuffing, represent the Podhale region of Southern Poland, in the Tatra Mountains. The man's outfit, typical of that of a sheep herder, includes pants and a jacket of natural felted wool, a heavily embroidered vest with sheep's wool border, a white linen shirt, felt hat with shells (which on the doll are represented by white seed beads), and leather kierpce (slippers). The woman's outfit includes a printed silk flowered skirt (that is modelled on an original costume skirt which would have been made of wool), an embroidered vest with a tie at the bottom, a white linen shirt, a cotton kerchief and leather kierpce. The faces of the dolls are hand painted on fabric.

ACCESSION NUMBER: 3.00 & 4.00
CRAFTSPERSON: Unknown
DIMENSIONS: 55.5cm (h) female doll,
    57.5cm (h) male doll
MATERIALS: wool, silk, linen, cotton, seed beads,
    and leather
DATE: 1933

2. KNITTED SLIPPERS

These grey/brown slippers with red and navy blue designs are typical of the socks and slippers found in Eastern and Central Europe. MANITOBA CRAFTS MUSEUM AND LIBRARY records indicate that they are from Albania, but the slippers also have very pointed toes, showing a Turkish influence. Slippers of this type were very popular during the early to mid-20th century.

ACCESSION NUMBER: 8.00 & 8.01
CRAFTSPERSON: Unknown
DIMENSIONS: 23cm (l) x 10.5cm (w) x 7 cm (h)
MATERIALS: wool dyed with alkaline dyes
DATE: Early 20th Century

3. TURNED BOWL

This bowl was turned on a lathe, likely in the 1930s. It is beautiful in its simplicity of form and lack of embellishment. The craftsperson was obviously quite skillful, and is known to us only as Mrs. Hinds.

ACCESSION NUMBER: 30.00
CRAFTSPERSON: Mrs. Hinds
DIMENSIONS: 24.5cm (dia) x 12.5cm (h)
MATERIALS: poplar
DATE: 1930s

4. AYRSHIRE EMBROIDERED CHILD'S DRESS

Embellished with Ayrshire embroidery, this little dress, in all probability, would have originally been a christening gown. The long skirt was shortened at the top so that the embroidery begins immediately below the bodice. Both the floral designs and embroidery techniques that feature padded satin stitches, eyelets, various counted thread fillings, and French knots, to name a few, are executed on very fine fabric. This delicate Scottish embroidery technique dates from approximately 1812 – 14 when the Napoleonic wars created a blockade on French laces.

At this time a Mrs. Jamieson, wife of an Ayr cotton agent, decided she could copy the designs and lace-like embroidery of a child's robe made in France and loaned to her by a Lady Mary Montgomery. Along with her daughters, Mrs. Jamieson very quickly organized a cottage industry of some 80,000 embroiderers at its peak. Both Scottish and Irish rural women eked out a living in most often wretched surroundings by embroidering robes, women's caps, handkerchiefs and baby's attire, which entailed both piecework and complete items. The industry flourished until the mid 1800s when the invention of the Swiss embroidery machine was able to more quickly produce similar results and the outbreak of the American Civil War in 1861 limited the export of the fine muslin required for Ayrshire work.

ACCESSION NUMBER: 37.00
CRAFTSPERSON: Unknown
DIMENSIONS: 45cm (l)
MATERIALS: white muslin, cotton thread
DATE: Early 19th Century

5. EMBROIDERED BELL PULL

This bell pull, fashioned like a sampler that would be used as a reference for future projects, was undoubtedly designed and embroidered by members of the CRAFTS GUILD OF MANITOBA to showcase some of the fifteen ethnic groups within the GUILD. Subsequently, the many embroidery techniques they practised were also taught at the GUILD. The embroidered samples include Hardanger embroidery from Norway, Jacobean and crewel, best associated with English and East Indian work, Ukrainian embroidery from the Bukovyna region, Hungarian embroidery that reflects the Transylvania area, and white stitch work on black satin weave cloth, also a Hungarian technique found on the national costume during the 19th century. Recognized as a unique and very meaningful embroidery at the Canadian National Exhibition, it received a $10 special mention award.

Because it was a project of the GUILD's EMBROIDERY GROUP, this bell pull was automatically placed in the PERMANENT COLLECTION.

ACCESSION NUMBER: 47.00
CRAFTSPERSON: Members of the Embroidery Group of the Crafts Guild of Manitoba: Mitzi Anderson Dale, Mrs. Zola Istvanffy, Mrs. G.D. Juettner, Mrs. W.M. Hugill, Mrs. F. Howorth, Mrs. P. Hutzulak, Mrs. W. Larsson, Mrs. M. Whitworth, Mrs. H. Wilson, and Mrs. F. Young.
DIMENSIONS: 12.5cm (w) x 119cm (l)
MATERIALS: satin, cotton, wool, canvas, silk and artificial fibres
DATE: 1930s

6. WOVEN WALL HANGING

This wool tapestry was purchased by the GUILD in 1933. While the name of the craftsperson is not known, the technique is used in all the Scandinavian countries. The text, in Danish, reads "5 KLOGE JOMFRUER / 5 DAARLIGE JOMFRUER", or in English "5 Wise Virgins / 5 Bad Virgins". When the front of the wall hanging is showing, the letters appear in the right order from left to right, but reversed. This is because, tapestries are woven with the back side facing the weaver, and the maker forgot to weave the letters in reverse.

The tapestry illustrates the parable of the five wise and five foolish virgins from Matthew 25:1-13. The wise virgins on the top line have oil lamps to guide their men home in the night. Narrative textiles such as this were first used in Viking times as burial shrouds depicting figures from Norse mythology and then later the same techniques were used for Christian subjects. The subject of the wise and foolish virgins is most common in Norway.

ACCESSION NUMBER: 48.00
CRAFTSPERSON: Unknown
TRANSLATED FROM DANISH BY Karen Jacks
DIMENSIONS: 126cm (w) x 147cm (l)
MATERIALS: wool
DATE: c. 1930

7. BUFFALO HAIR MITTENS, SCARF AND MAT

In 1942 at the height of the Second World War, a group of women from the CRAFTS GUILD OF MANITOBA completed an experiment in alternative fibres. During the war, sheep's wool was being used almost exclusively by the Canadian Armed Forces to produce warm clothing for the troops, leaving little for craftspeople. So Kitty Churchill, Agnes McTaggart, and Flora McIvor undertook to test buffalo hair as a replacement. After getting permission to pick fleece off of the fences at the Assiniboine Park Zoo, these women cleaned, carded, spun and dyed 1.5 pounds of fleece. Some was mixed with sheep's wool. The women completed three pieces – a pair of knitted mittens, a small hooked mat, and a woven scarf.

Although it was possible to use the bison fibre, it was not deemed a good replacement for sheep's wool. It was both difficult to collect and also quite resistant to dyes.

While the experiment did not result in a new source of fibres it did illustrate the extent to which resourcefulness was a part of Canadian wartime life.

ACCESSION NUMBER: 54.00, 55.00, 56.00
CRAFTSPERSON: Flora McIvor, Agnes McTaggart
    and Kitty Churchill
DIMENSIONS: Scarf #54.00: 26.5cm (w) x 120.00cm (l);
    Mittens #55.00: 11cm (w) x 31cm (l);
    Mat #56: 20cm (dia)
MATERIALS: buffalo wool, sheep's wool, natural dyes
DATE: 1942

8. BEADED MOCCASINS

These moccasins are from the Northern Plains region of North America and were likely made by a Plains Cree, Dakota/Sioux or Stoney woman in the early part of the 20th century. Although it is difficult to determine the exact cultural origins of pieces like this, the side seam construction does point to a Stoney origin. The beaded motifs are more Plains Cree or Dakota/Sioux.

The leather is brain tanned moose hide and the beads are glass. The seams are sewn with cotton thread. All the beadwork is done in an appliqué technique, where one thread holds the beads and a second thread tacks the first thread down every two or three beads. Many moccasins are beaded using a "lazy stitch", whereby a single thread is brought up through the leather, four to six beads are strung onto this thread, and it is then sewn back down. This method is continued in rows of beads with the result that the pattern appears to be rows of beaded sections, and the beads are raised slightly off of the leather.

ACCESSION NUMBER: 58.00
CRAFTSPERSON: Unknown
DIMENSIONS: 9.5cm (w) x 18.5cm (h) x 24.7cm (l)
MATERIALS: moose hide, seed beads, cotton thread
DATE: 1890 – 1930

9. BEADED MITTENS

These mittens have a charming feature – a small beaded flower on the thumb of each hand. The beadwork is exquisite and uses a variety of bead sizes, including some that are less than 1mm wide. Also incorporated into the design are strategically placed metallic beads, most with faceted sides.

The silk ribbon work marks these mittens as being made by the Dene speaking people, but the beadwork has strong Métis characteristics, so these mittens likely originated with the Cree or Cree-Métis people from northern Manitoba.

ACCESSION NUMBER: 62.00
CRAFTSPERSON: Unknown
DIMENSIONS: 14cm (w) x 28.7cm (l)
MATERIALS: leather, glass & copper beads, silk ribbon, wool, cotton thread
DATE: c. 1870

10. HOOKED WILDFLOWER RUG

Eleven of Manitoba's wildflowers are depicted on this hooked rug. They are from the top left: tiger lily, wild rose and cone flower, clover, columbine and iris, lady slipper, vetch and tiger lily (pictured twice), and Indian paint brush, crocus and goldenrod.

The rug was made by the Rug Hooking Group of the Crafts Guild of Manitoba. Groups like this regularly undertook projects to commemorate events or just to have fun. This particular rug was made using wool yarn rather than strips of used clothing.

ACCESSION NUMBER: 70.00
CRAFTSPERSON: Rug Hooking Group at the Crafts Guild of Manitoba, organized by Agnes McTaggart
DIMENSIONS: 145cm (l) x 216 cm (w)
MATERIALS: wool, jute
DATE: 1940s

11. WOVEN WALL HANGING

Teaching rural women to make decorative art for their homes so that *"the eye is not tired by ugliness"* was one of the concerns of the designer and weaver of this tapestry, Mitzi Anderson Dale. She was born in Oslo, Norway and came to Canada in 1926. As a member of the CRAFTS GUILD OF MANITOBA, she taught classes on weaving and dyeing with natural dyes found in the area. The tapestry, woven of vegetable-dyed wool, was done in 1931 on an upright loom.

Mitzi Dale Anderson's designs were inspired by Norse legend and a landscape of waves and mountains and conical trees, according to an article, *"A Winnipeg Album"*, in the Manitoba Archives. She left Winnipeg in 1933 to move to Toronto.

ACCESSION NUMBER: 78.00
TITLE: *TYSISE BLAAUEIS ALF/DANSER I MANENATTEN*
    Tysise blue anemone fairy/dances in the blue moonlit night
TRANSLATED FROM NORWEGIAN BY: Laverne Carlson
CRAFTSPERSON: Mitzi Anderson Dale
DIMENSIONS: 49cm (w) x 50cm (l)
MATERIALS: wool
DATE: 1933

12. RED RIVER APPLIQUÉ QUILT

This group project was undertaken by the EMBROIDERY GROUP at the CRAFTS GUILD OF MANITOBA to celebrate the history of the Red River Settlement in Manitoba. The quilt squares include HBC Lower Fort Garry, the Countess of Dufferin (the first locomotive in Manitoba), the St. Boniface Cathedral, St. Andrews Church, a sod hut and pioneer cottage, an ox cart, and some of the people of the region including the pioneers, the Selkirk settlers and the Aboriginal inhabitants. The centre square depicts both the past and present (as of 1945) Winnipeg with the tepees juxtaposed with the modern buildings of Winnipeg.

The names of those involved with the making of the quilt are embroidered on the reverse.

ACCESSION NUMBER: 102.00

TITLE: *Red River Quilt*

CRAFTSPERSON: Designed by Sophia May Osborne. The top was appliquéd and embroidered by the members of the EMBROIDERY GROUP AT THE CRAFTS GUILD OF MANITOBA. Specifically: Lower Fort Garry –A. Lowe and M. Newman, Countess of Dufferin –Phoebe E. Heise, Sod Hut –E. Green and E.H. Scrimshaw, Aboriginal People –Anne Dowton, St. Boniface Cathedral –V. Harvey, Historic Objects –Verna Ayre, J. Horne, Eunice Young and A.R. McLaren, Dream Scene in Centre –P. Sawyer, Anne Dowton, Lyla G. Hugill, Pioneers –Lyla G. Hugill, Ox Cart –M.J. Stone, Pioneers Cottage –M.J. Stone and E. Green, Selkirk Settlers –K.M. Fayden Radford, St. Andrews Church –Flora Marshall. The quilting was also completed by Mrs. R. Wilson, M.A. Young, M.A. Whitworth, Mary MacLeod, Catherine Whitelaw, E. Robinson, M.L. Phair, Jennie B. Webb, J. Skelton, Helen Cunningham, V.R. Atha, R. Hilda Gillespie, Laura McHugh, Selina Lawrence, and R. Ashmore.

DIMENSIONS: 191cm (w) x 218cm (l)

MATERIALS: cotton fabric, cotton embroidery floss, quilt batting unknown.

DATE: 1945 – 1946

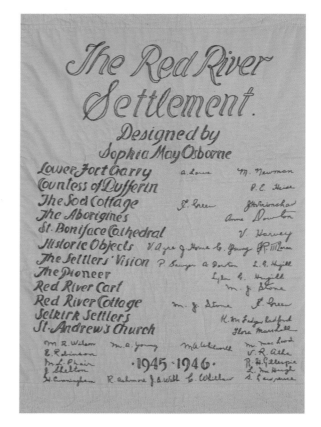

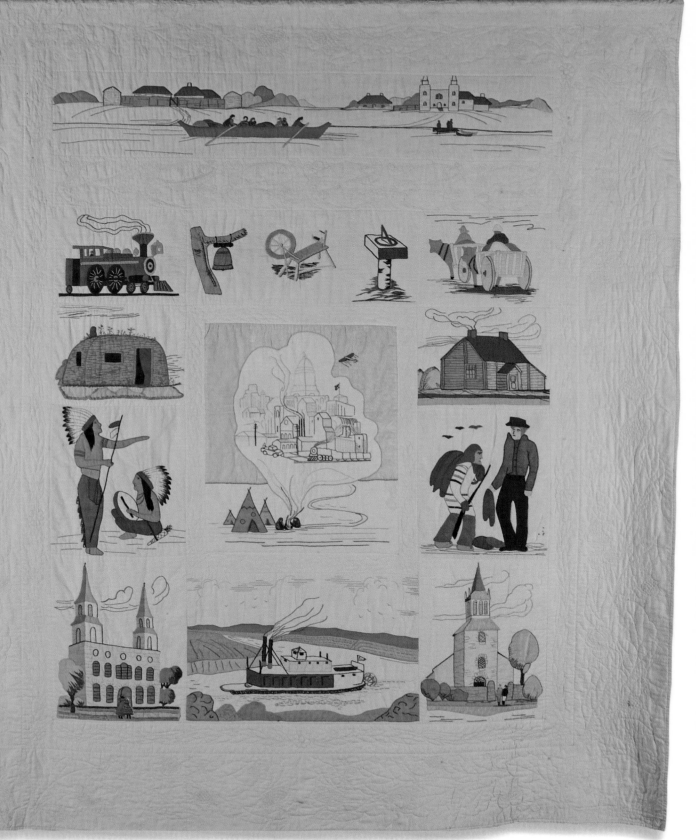

13. CERAMIC FIGURINE

In the present day, Leo Mol is one of Manitoba's best known artists, mainly for his large bronze sculptures and stained glass windows. However, during his early years in Winnipeg it was smaller ceramic pieces that were his initial best sellers.

Born in Polonne, Ukraine, in 1915, Mol spent his early years learning the art of ceramics from his father. As a young adult he studied first in Leningrad, and later Berlin. In 1943 he married Margareth and in 1945 as Russian troops moved in to the city, the couple escaped from Berlin. After a few years in the Netherlands, Mol and his wife moved to Canada.

Once in Winnipeg he contacted the CRAFTS GUILD OF MANITOBA, where volunteers suggested that he make pieces that were a reflection of life in Canada. Thus he began a series of ceramic pieces that included a beaver, robin, Inuit hunter, lumberjack, and this pair of square dancers. They sold for a very reasonable $15 each in the early 1950s.

ACCESSION NUMBER: 109.00
CRAFTSPERSON: Leo Mol
DIMENSIONS: 26.4 cm (h) x 12.5cm (w)
MATERIALS: Manitoba clay, glaze
DATE: 1953

14. SUGAR BOWL AND CREAMER

As a husband and wife team, Erica and Kjeld Deichmann produced pottery pieces in their New Brunswick studio from 1934, when they immigrated to Canada from Denmark, until 1963 when Kjeld died suddenly. Kjeld specialized in throwing the pots, and Erica worked on the glazing, so most pieces were truly a shared effort. Their work is highly respected.

This delicate creamer and sugar bowl were donated in memory of Gladys Chown, former president of the CRAFTS GUILD OF MANITOBA.

ACCESSION NUMBER: 114.06 & 114.07
CRAFTSPERSON: Erica and Kjeld Deichmann
DIMENSIONS: creamer 9.7cm (h) x 8.5cm (dia),
    sugar bowl 8cm (h) x 9cm (dia)
MATERIALS: clay, glaze
DATE: c. 1940

15. COILED SALISH BASKET

To make this basket, Salish women from the Fraser and Thompson River area of British Columbia would dig cedar roots approximately four to five meters away from a tree. After digging into the ground with a hardwood stick the women would select roots with a 2.5cm diameter and pull these up by hand. Those roots found in the muddy banks of the Fraser River were preferred. The outer coverings were then stripped off and the root itself was then split in two. To make a basket the roots were sewn closely in a continuous row over a flat foundation of cedar slats. The wooden slat was pierced close to the top edge with an awl to allow the root to pass through. The chequered design on the side is created with strips of cherry bark. The red colour is natural. The black is achieved by burying the bark in the black mud, sometimes with iron nails, to deepen the colour.

This basketry technique known as "beading" creates rows of alternately exposed and concealed stitches on the basket wall.

ACCESSION NUMBER: 134.00
CRAFTSPERSON: Unknown
DIMENSIONS: 9.5 cm (w) x 6.8cm (h) x 14.5cm (l)
MATERIALS: split cedar root, cedar wood slats, cherry bark, natural dyes
DATE: Early – Mid 20th Century

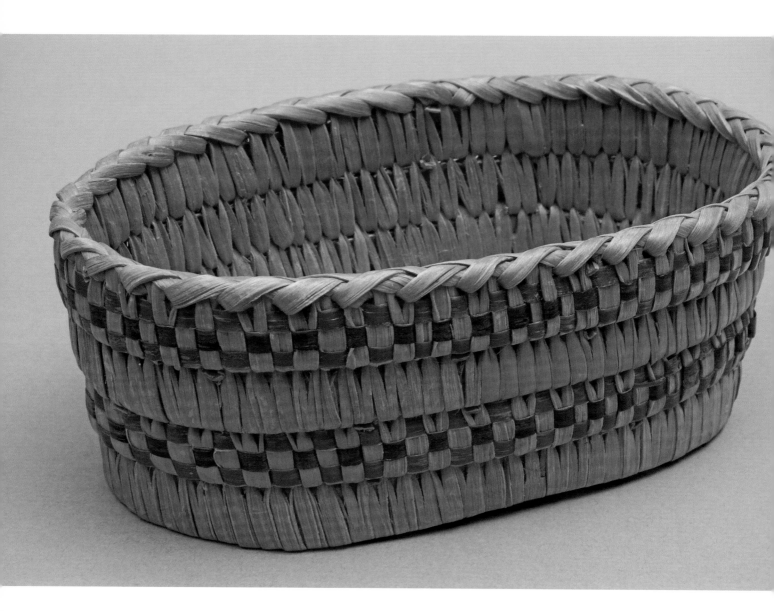

16. TWINED ALEUT BASKET

This delicate twined basket was made by a woman in the Aleutian Islands area using local Northwest Coast grasses and silk embroidery thread. Such baskets were likely made for sale to tourists and were designed to hold trinkets and other small items.

ACCESSION NUMBER: 135.00
CRAFTSPERSON: Unknown
DIMENSIONS: basket 14cm (h) x 16cm (dia), lid 7cm (h) x 16.5cm (dia)
MATERIALS: split grasses, silk embroidery floss
DATE: Late 19ᵗʰ Century – 1940s

17. FAMOUS NAMES SIGNATURE QUILT

The Second World War years were characterized by endless fundraising projects, mainly by the women left at home, to support the troops fighting overseas. In Toronto, the Air Force Officers' Wives, led by Margaret Bishop, wife of World War I Flying Ace Billy Bishop, began an ambitious project that came to be known as the Famous Names Quilt.

The project began with the collection of over 1,100 signatures, many of famous people. Signatures were collected at Air Force Bases where both the entertainers such as Bob Hope, Lucille Ball, Hedy Lamarr and James Cagney signed the fabric, along with many servicemen from Allied countries including Canada, the United States, New Zealand, England, Australia, and Poland. Other fabric squares were signed by the Dionne quintuplets, Winston Churchill and his immediate entourage, Mackenzie King, and various sororities. It is suspected that Billy Bishop facilitated this during his many speaking tours.

The signatures were embroidered by the women of the Air Force Officers' Wives. The squares were then assembled and quilted by Sisters of the Good Shepherd in Ottawa.

Raffle tickets to win the quilt were sold and a woman from Manitoba won. She then sold tickets to a tea in her home with the money raised going to the war effort. In 1955 Mrs. Wengel donated the quilt to the PERMANENT COLLECTION.

ACCESSION NUMBER: 142.00
TITLE: Famous Names Quilt
CRAFTSPERSON: Quilt organized by Mrs. Margaret Bishop – wife of WWI Flying Ace Billy Bishop. Embroidered by the women of the Air Force Officers' Wives in Toronto. Quilted by the Sisters of the Good Shepherd in Ottawa.
DIMENSIONS: 243cm (w) x 273cm (l)
MATERIALS: cotton, quilt batting unknown
DATE: 1940 – 42

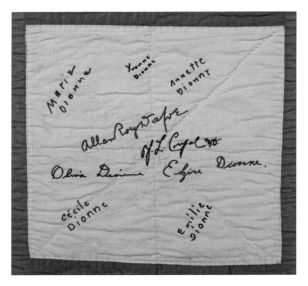

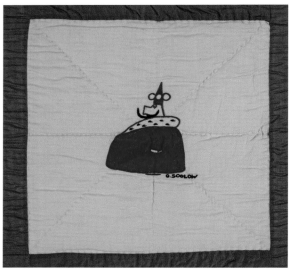

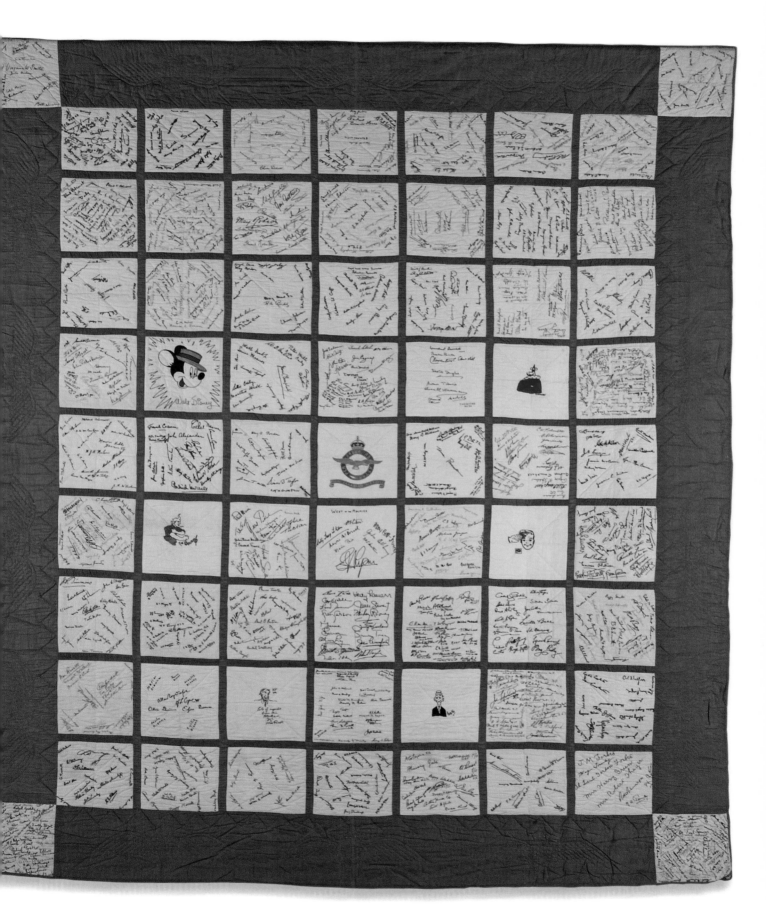

18. WALRUS CARVING

The Canadian Handicrafts Guild - Manitoba Branch, along with the main branch in Montreal, was instrumental in the initial recognition and marketing of Inuit art in the early 1950s. In cooperation with James Houston of the Hudson's Bay Company, the Guild shipped sculptures from the remote northern communities to Montreal and Winnipeg for sale to a southern market.

Large wooden shipping crates packed with the carvings arrived in Winnipeg. A small shed behind the Guild's building was used for unpacking and sorting. Twice a year, these carvings were sold to art lovers in Manitoba. The line-up for this sale usually stretched around the block!

The prices for these carvings were very reasonable, with some available for as little as $5. But the Guild kept only 20-30% of the total sale with the rest being sent back to the artists. Despite this small commission, the sale of the Inuit work often made up a significant portion of the total Guild sales. In 1966 alone the profit was $12,000!

This walrus from Inukjuak (formerly Port Harrison), carved from serpentine, with tusks of ivory and soap inlay eyes, is typical of many carvings from the 1950s.

ACCESSION NUMBER: 152.00
CRAFTSPERSON: Unknown
DIMENSIONS: 14cm (w) x 13.3 cm (h) x 38.1cm (l)
MATERIALS: serpentine, soap, and ivory
DATE: c. 1955

19. KAYAK CARVING

This green serpentine kayak, with Inuit hunter, seal
float, paddle and hunting tools is from the community
of Kimmirut (formerly Lake Harbour), Baffin Island.

ACCESSION NUMBER: 183.00
CRAFTSPERSON: Possibly Sheokjuk Oqutak
DIMENSIONS: 5.6cm (w) x 13.3cm (h) x 30.2cm (l)
MATERIALS: serpentine, ivory, India ink, sinew
DATE: 1952 – 1959

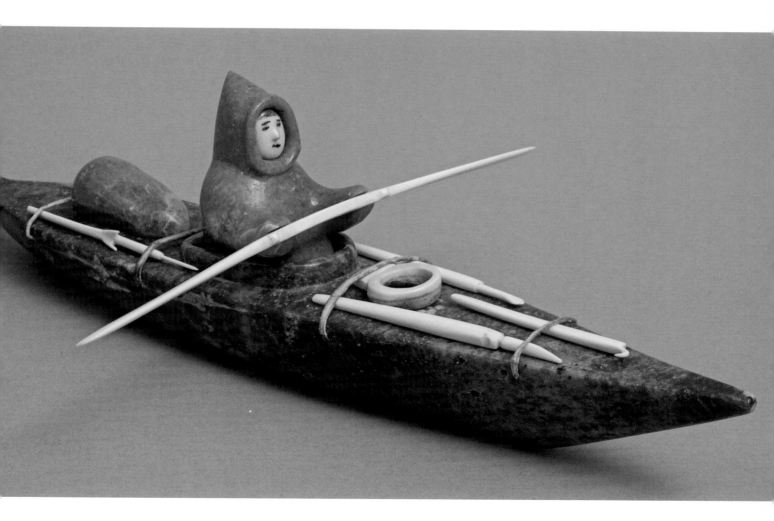

20. MANITOBA TARTAN SCARF

The Manitoba Tartan was co-designed by Hugh and Dorothy Rankine, long-standing members of the GUILD, who presented it at the Guild's Annual General Meeting on April 7, 1958. The tartan is registered in Scotland by the guardian of Scottish heraldry and was accepted as an official provincial symbol in the Legislature under Bill No. 126. April 6th was declared by The Queen to be Manitoba Tartan Day.

The blue lines of the tartan represent Lord Selkirk's Hamilton blood, the dark red squares represent the Red River settlement, the green squares represent the province's natural resources, the yellow lines represent the grains which are vital to the Province's economy, and the green lines represent the men and women of different cultures who have enriched the life of the Province.

The scarf was woven on a twill threading using wool that was coloured with alkaline dyes. It was one of the very first pieces of Manitoba tartan woven, and it was immediately donated to the permanent collection.

ACCESSION NUMBER: 190.00
CRAFTSPERSON: Elsie Ogston
DIMENSIONS: 30cm (w) x 138cm (l)
MATERIALS: wool
DATE: 1958

21. GOLD EMBROIDERY

Typical of material from northern India, this black wool and gold silk cloth is embroidered in silk embroidery floss and gold thread wrapped around a silk core. Both the wool and the cream coloured silk are embroidered in stylized designs that could be either carnations or peacocks. Although Turkish and Indian gold work are similar, this embroidery is notably Indian in that the gold thread wrapped around a core of silk is used as opposed to the Turkish gold wire that is couched to the background fabric. Because it is heavily embellished and not all glitter, the cloth appears not to be a regular tourist piece, but may have been created for an aristocrat who would have placed his hookah pipe or brass urn on it. It might also have been a tablecloth, hanging, cushion or mirror cover. The stains on the lining suggest that the piece was used in a functional manner, but it is also possible that a piece of soiled silk was applied to the back of the cloth.

Research indicates it may have been created in Kashmir, one of the few places in India that uses wool, primarily because of the hilly terrain that is naturally cool. It might also have come from Uttar Pradesh, Andra Pradesh or Delhi. There are no records regarding the donor or history of this intriguing cloth.

ACCESSION NUMBER: 205.00
CRAFTSPERSON: Unknown
DIMENSIONS: 83.3cm (w) x 84cm (l)
MATERIALS: black wool, yellow silk, cream silk, cotton thread, silk embroidery floss, and gold thread wrapped around a core of silk embroidery thread.
DATE: c. Early 1900s

22. RED RIVER CART MODEL

For many years, this famous symbol of the Red River Settlement in Manitoba was sold at the GUILD Shop that carried various models made by several craftsmen. This particular one was made by Fred W. Alexander, likely in the 1940s or 1950s. The original full-size carts were constructed completely from wood. Due to the dusty ground it was impossible to use lubricants for the wheels, and as a result they could be heard approaching for miles. The North West Fiddle became their colourful nickname.

ACCESSION NUMBER: 212.00
CRAFTSPERSON: Fred W. Alexander
DIMENSIONS: 10.5cm (w) x 7.7cm (h) x 18.5cm (l)
MATERIALS: white pine
DATE: c. 1950

23. UKRAINIAN EMBROIDERED WOMAN'S SHIRT

There are many elements about this shirt that speak of the Ukraine and particularly the region of Sokal – the hand-woven fabric, wide "sailor" collar, and of course the embroidery, although it is a variation of the more traditional design that would feature black with bits of red or yellow. Each region of the Ukraine has its own particular type of costume and embroidery style that tends to remain much the same so that people are easily identified as to their place of origin. The buttons on this shirt have replaced the red ribbon found on older shirts. Traditionally three bands of embroidery were used on the sleeves. Men's shirts were embroidered down the front because their sleeves were covered with a jacket; women's shirts were embroidered on the collar and sleeves with the torso being covered by a vest. The embroidered designs on this shirt include poppies and bachelor buttons, two of the most popular motifs. Beautiful as it is, this shirt would have been worn as an everyday garment as the fabric was considered inferior in comparison to white linen.

This shirt was likely fashioned by a Ukrainian woman who immigrated to Canada. Before marriage every woman would prepare a dowry chest with many shirts, including the one in which she would be buried.

ACCESSION NUMBER: 225.00
CRAFTSPERSON: Unknown
DIMENSIONS: 70cm (l)
MATERIALS: hand-woven linen, embroidery floss
DATE: c. 1930s

24. WHALEBONE CARVING

This carving has not been attributed to a specific carver, but likely originates from Naujat (formerly Repulse Bay). Unusual in that it is completely whalebone (except for a small piece of antler used to make one of the pegs holding the bird to the base), as opposed to stone, it depicts a pair of arctic birds, possibly terns, tending to a nest with two eggs.

ACCESSION NUMBER: 236.00
CRAFTSPERSON: Unknown
DIMENSIONS: 11cm (w) x 11.5cm (h) x 19.5cm (l)
MATERIALS: whalebone, antler
DATE: after 1948

25. SEALSKIN WALL HANGING

This sealskin hanging from Killiniq (formerly Port Burwell) is an amazing feat of sewing. The scenes, depicting life inside the igloo, a man and woman in traditional clothing, a modern house, a caribou, a variety of dogs, a fox and birds, are all inset using tiny whip stitches into the background. Some individual pieces, such as the details on the parkas, are less than 1cm wide. Great skill was needed to sew the tiny pieces together and still have the whole piece lie flat.

It is believed that the production of skin pieces for sale was discouraged due to the strong smell that results from the natural processing of the seal hides. As a result, this type of work is rare.

ACCESSION NUMBER: 261.00
CRAFTSPERSON: Emily Annatuk
DIMENSIONS: 261cm (w) x 110 cm (h)
MATERIALS: sealskin, sinew
DATE: c. 1950s

26. WOVEN PLACEMAT

This placemat was donated by Flora Marshall and was created as an educational piece for weaving classes at the GUILD. The lacy weave and the use of a combination of blue and yellow threads results in the woven piece appearing green, except in the open pattern areas where the blue weft can be seen distinctly.

ACCESSION NUMBER: 268.08
CRAFTSPERSON: Unknown
DIMENSIONS: 26cm (w) x 33cm (l)
MATERIALS: cotton
DATE: 1950 – 1960

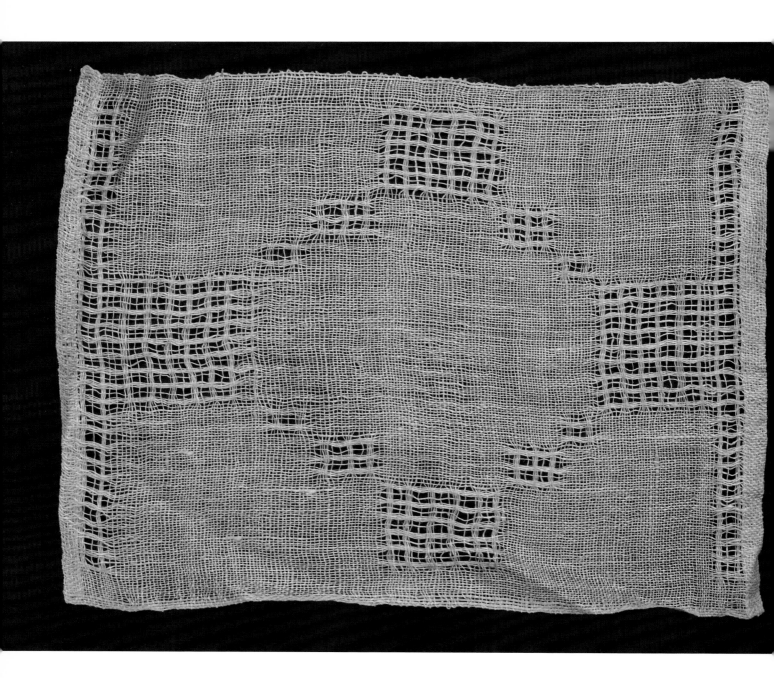

27. WOVEN APRON

The design on this apron is woven in Dukagång, a finger-manipulated or laid-in technique that has been highly developed in Sweden and is seen throughout the Scandinavian countries. The pattern threads lie on the surface of a plain-weave background and are tied down by every fourth warp thread. Designs, such as the figures on the apron, are usually very stylized.

This apron was woven by Inga McGougan, and it was donated to the collection of the CRAFTS MUSEUM AND LIBRARY by the artist.

ACCESSION NUMBER: 310.00
CRAFTSPERSON: Inga McGougan
DIMENSIONS: 35cm (w) x 47cm (l)
MATERIALS: synthetic fibres
DATE: c. 1950

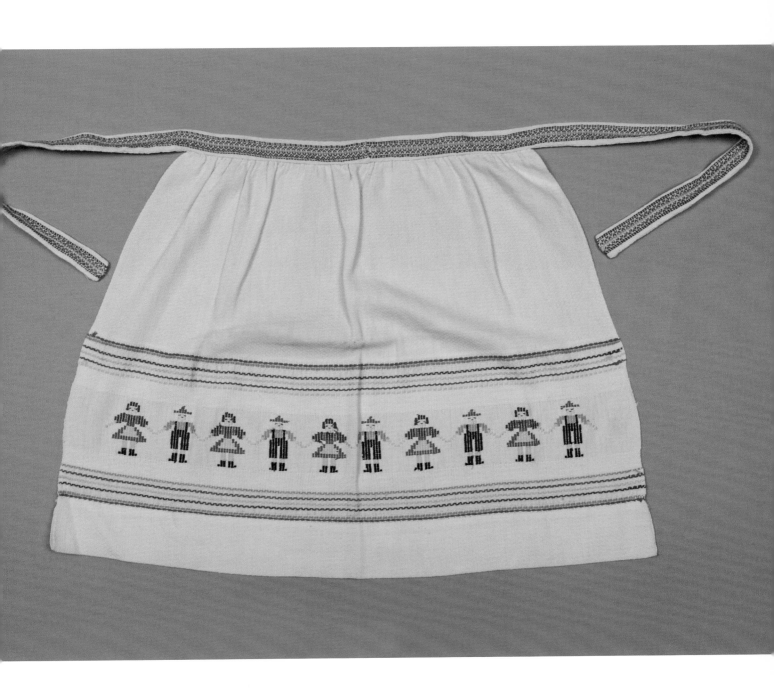

28. "GREEN WOMAN" CARVING

In the oral history of the CRAFTS GUILD OF MANITOBA, this carving was affectionately called the *"Green Woman"*. She spent many years on display and was loved by many GUILD members. Unusual in her size, 65 cm tall, she was one of the first pieces made after a green stone quarry near Kingat (formerly Cape Dorset) was located in 1964.

Note: There are alternate spellings of the artist's name, including Mannumi, Manome, Manomee, Munamee, Munameekota.

ACCESSION NUMBER: 316.00
CRAFTSPERSON: Manumi Shaqu
DIMENSIONS: 65cm (h)
MATERIALS: serpentine
DATE: c. 1964 – 1970

29. EMBROIDERED 1825 SAMPLER

In all likelihood, Margaret Hay, during her early elementary school years would have stitched this sampler in the classroom under the watchful eye of her teacher. While Margaret was born in Northern Ireland, samplers such as this were created in schools throughout numerous European countries and North America during the 18th and 19th centuries. In most cases, the children were already well acquainted with both the alphabets and numbers they stitched. The samplers were meant to help young girls hone their embroidery skills in preparation for marriage or careers as servants when they would be expected to mark and identify the household linens with embroidered initials.

It is thought that this sampler was given to the donor, Frances O'Grady, in 1886, when she and other family members visited Margaret Hay in Glasgow.

ACCESSION NUMBER: 356.00
CRAFTSPERSON: Margaret Hay,
    who later became Margaret Dale
DIMENSIONS: 16.9cm (w) x 13.9cm (h)
MATERIALS: evenweave linen, 70 threads to the inch,
    embroidery floss, bamboo frame with glass
DATE: 1825

30. CHINESE BATIK WALL HANGING

This Chinese Batik, specifically from the Hmong or Miao culture, was likely used to celebrate a marriage. The many symbols of longevity and good luck point to this use.

The centre design is a water lily, representing purity, serenity and peace. Around this are 26 petals of the lily that represent "one hundred harmonies". The two birds are phoenixes that are arranged to form a yin-yang symbol. There is a peony flower beside the wing of each bird that symbolizes good fortune and the promise of an extended family. Between the two rows of dots in the circle are $44^{1}/_{2}$ peaches, symbolizing longevity and

good wishes. There is a lotus blossom in each of the four corners. Between the two rows of dots in the square are ancient utensils for drinking, often used as ritual objects in tombs, and signifying balance and stability. The motif around the edge is peaches. The circle motif in the batik represents heaven while the square symbolizes the earthly realm.

The designs were made using wooden blocks and the wax-resist technique known as batik.

ACCESSION NUMBER: 366.00
CRAFTSPERSON: Unknown
DIMENSIONS: 74cm (w) x 71.5cm (l)
MATERIALS: cotton
DATE: 20th Century

31. QUILLWORK BELT

Before the arrival of Europeans and their glass beads, Aboriginal people in Canada often created decorated panels like this using porcupine quills. The hollow quills can be easily flattened and dyed using natural dyes. Belts such as this one are woven on a bow loom.

This belt was made by a Dene woman, likely from the Northern area of Manitoba or Saskatchewan.

ACCESSION NUMBER: 369.00
CRAFTSPERSON: Unknown
DIMENSIONS: 4cm (w) x 68.2cm (l)
MATERIALS: porcupine quills, black velvet, cotton thread,
   glass beads, alkaline dyes
DATE: c. 1850

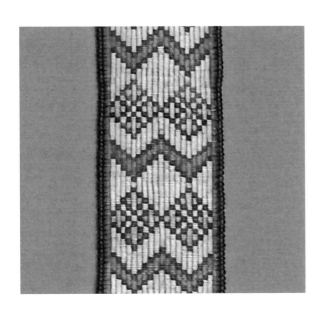

32. CRAZY QUILT

Crazy Quilts became very popular in the late Victorian Era, especially among more well-to-do ladies. The small scraps of velvet, silk and other fabrics made a rich and varied appearance. The sometimes extensive embroidery and embellishment created a unique look and an opportunity for the quilt maker to truly customize the quilt.

Sarah P. Hamm was 30 years old when she made this quilt that includes illustrations from Kate Greenaway, an English illustrator of children's books.

ACCESSION NUMBER: 377.00
CRAFTSPERSON: Sarah P. Hamm
DIMENSIONS: 138cm (w) x 183cm (l)
MATERIALS: silk, velvet, felt, cotton, embroidery thread,
    quilt batting
DATE: 1882

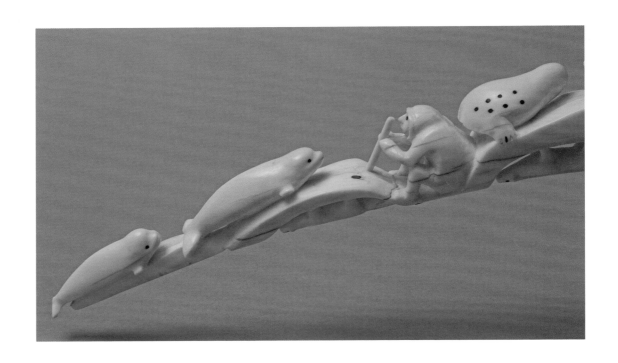

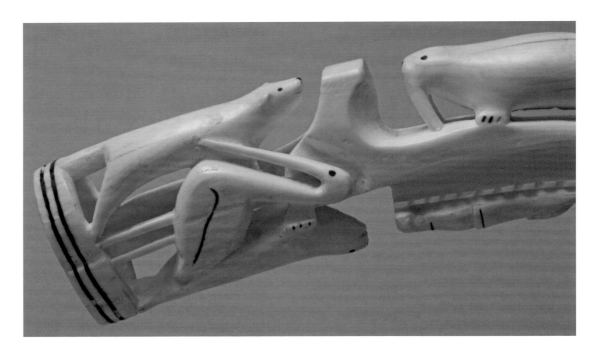

33. CARVED WALRUS TUSK

During the early years of the Inuit carving trade in the south, Inuit artists were given numbers by the trading posts, their Inuit names being too difficult to record. This resulted in cases where art work has been misidentified. In this case, the number and the syllabic on the piece refer to Simeonie Weetaluktuk, but our research indicates that this might not be correct. Simeonie was primarily a hunter, but his two brothers, Eli and Sarolie were accomplished carvers. However, if it were Simeonie who took the piece to the trading post, he might have put his name and number on the piece in order to get paid.

Regardless of the carver, this piece is very well executed. The carving covers the entire tusk and each side shows a different set of figures. A variety of animals, including beluga whales, walrus, bear, seals, sea birds, and foxes, along with a hunter and his sled, are depicted on the carving.

The dark inlay on the carving is made from melted long-play records.

ACCESSION NUMBER: 424.00
CRAFTSPERSON: Simeonie Weetaluktuk
DIMENSIONS: 5.7cm (w) x 13.3cm (h) x 49.5cm (l)
MATERIALS: walrus ivory, stone, antler,
    melted long play records
DATE: c. 1952

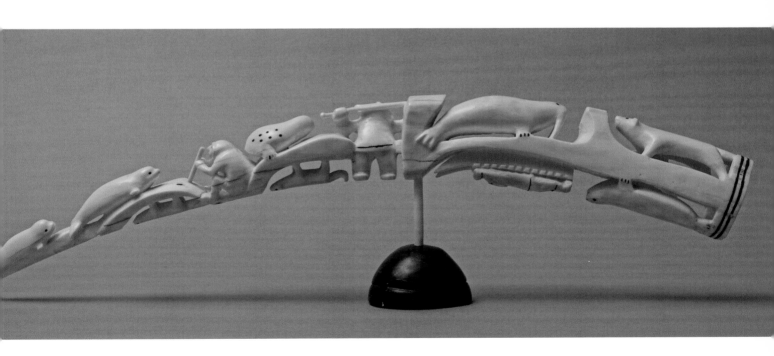

34. MACRAMÉ SCREEN

In 1970 the Province of Manitoba celebrated its Centennial, and the CRAFTS GUILD OF MANITOBA was not one to be left out of the events. At the height of macramé's popularity this screen was one of the projects made by GUILD Members to mark that significant year. The following year the macramé screen was selected for Manitoba Mainstream, a regional art exhibit, sponsored by the National Art Gallery in Ottawa and coordinated by the Winnipeg Art Gallery. The show travelled across the country from Nova Scotia to British Columbia.

Although the work was mainly done collectively by the Macramé Group, two panels were worked completely by Gerdine Crawford Strong. Specifically, these are the center panel and the panel at the lower left that includes the date and the CRAFTS GUILD OF MANITOBA initials.

ACCESSION NUMBER: 429.00
CRAFTSPERSON: The CRAFT GUILD OF MANITOBA MACRAME GROUP, convened by Selina Lawrence. Worked by Margaret Mitchell, Shirley Tyderkie, Gerdine Crawford Strong, Henrietta Mullin, Rose Brewster, Margaret Profit, Mary Carstens, Gladys Manson, Rheba Anderson, Louise Brown, Margaret Knudson, Elsie Rochelle, Charlotte Shuttleworth, Margaret Grant and Eleanor Melville.
DIMENSIONS: 144cm (w) x 163cm (h)
MATERIALS: hemp, cotton, wood, stain, metal hinges, fishing line, nails
DATE: 1970

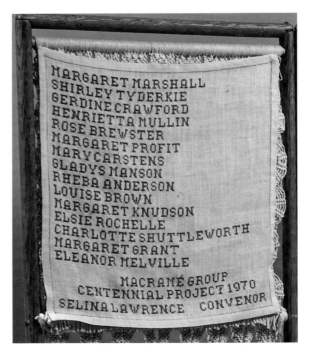

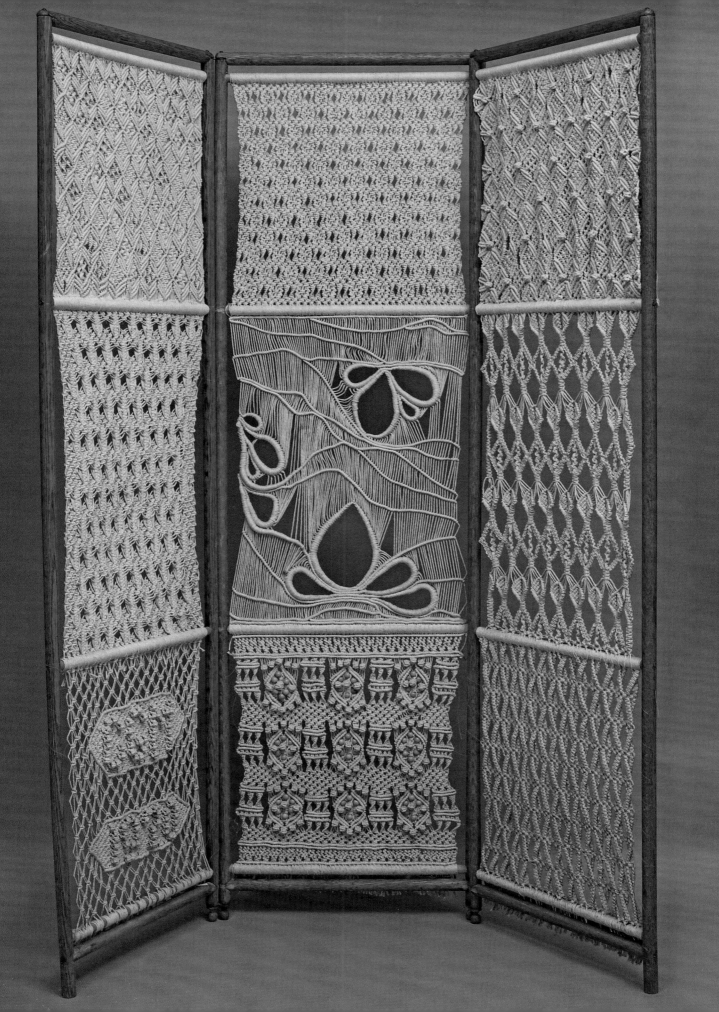

35. KNITTED BEADED BAG

As incredible as it may seem, all the beads in this bag were threaded on the yarn at the beginning of the project and brought into the piece as the knitting progressed. The ribbon strap has been beaded to cover the join of the two ends. A small pocket on the inside is embellished with the maker's initials, which are difficult to decipher, but likely are A.E.E.

ACCESSION NUMBER: 512.00
CRAFTSPERSON: Unknown
DIMENSIONS: 15cm (w) x 17.5cm (l)
MATERIALS: steel cut beads, silk, grosgrain ribbon
DATE: Early 20th Century

36. VASE

Steve Repa was one of those individuals who are strongly rooted in a particular environment, which in his case was the Canadian prairies. Much of Repa's art, which includes both ceramics and paintings, shows signs of this connection to the land through the use of rich colours and classic forms.

ACCESSION NUMBER: 518.00
CRAFTSPERSON: Steven Repa
DIMENSIONS: 17.9cm (h) x 16.2cm (dia)
MATERIALS: terracotta with slip
DATE: c. 1960s

37. JENNY DOLL

Winnipeg born Judy Pilgrim Stewart began creating dolls in her early childhood. Her interest in Victorian England and Canada's early pioneers is often reflected in her work and this doll is a fine example of Stewart's eye for historical detail. Made in 1974 for the Winnipeg Centennial, this doll wears a dress of wool, hand woven by Doris King, with Manitoba crocuses embroidered on the bodice. Her collar is made of tatted lace, made by Elise Billyand, and the edge of her skirt was crocheted by Elizabeth Wiebe. Judy Stewart's series of Jenny Dolls are named after her daughter of the same name.

ACCESSION NUMBER: 520.00
TITLE: Jenny Doll
CRAFTSPERSON: Judy Stewart
DIMENSIONS: 62.5cm (l)
MATERIALS: wool, woven cloth, velvet ribbon,
   tatting, gesso, varnish, acrylic, metal
DATE: 1974

38. TATTED RUNNER

Like most lace, the history of tatting is shrouded in mystery. Tatting is made using only one stitch – the double stitch – and the complexity comes in how it is all linked together. This type of work has been done for centuries, but the actual craft of tatting using either a needle or a shuttle, only became popular in the 16th century.

This particular piece is made using seventy-seven medallions, all with two rings of buttonhole motifs. It was likely a dresser runner, being a bit fine for use on a table.

ACCESSION NUMBER: 523.00
CRAFTSPERSON: Ann Bering
DIMENSIONS: 23cm (w) x 80cm (l)
MATERIALS: cotton
DATE: Early 20th Century

39. STRAW BASKET

This small sewing or jewellery basket was made using a frame of wire, and woven over with straw. Most of the work is flat woven, but the handles and the edges are worked using a five straw plait. Although there is no recorded information about this basket, an almost identical basket in the MANITOBA MUSEUM collection was made on a Hutterite colony near Elie, Manitoba in 1945. This type of work is similar to baskets found in the Ukraine and other parts of Eastern Europe.

ACCESSION NUMBER: 578.00 & 578.01
CRAFTSPERSON: Unknown
DIMENSIONS: 19.7cm (w) x 14.5cm (h)
MATERIALS: straw, silk, wire
DATE: Mid 20th Century

40. IRISH CROCHET BAG

Irish Crochet is a distinctive type of crochet that results in a layered effect, usually using floral motifs. In the photograph the bag is stuffed with a small black pillow to show the detail in the work.

Irish Crochet is thought to have received its name in the potato famine era, when women earned a meagre living making this type of lace for use as edgings or as finished pieces like this bag.

ACCESSION NUMBER: 593.04
CRAFTSPERSON: Unknown
DIMENSIONS: 21.5cm (w) x 37cm (l)
MATERIALS: cotton
DATE: Late 19th Century

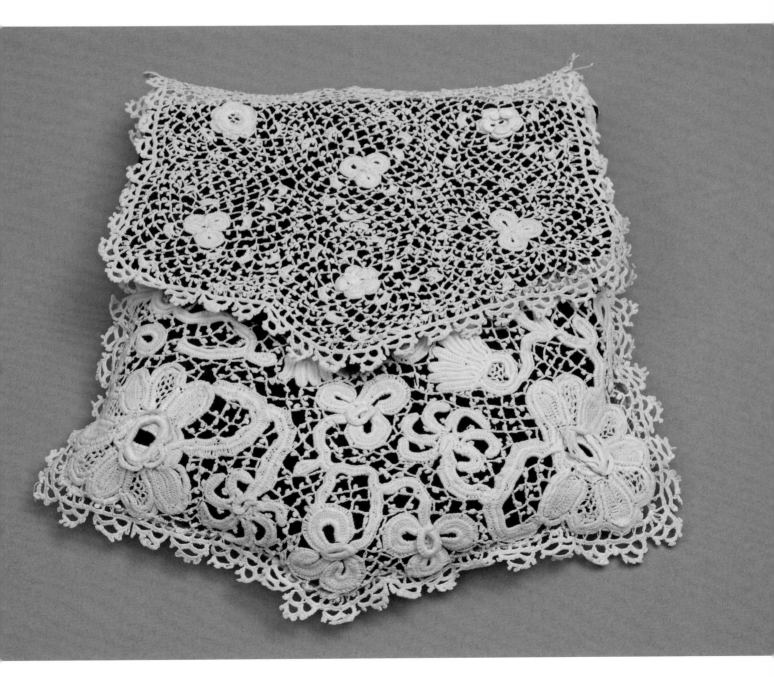

41. ECUADORIAN SPINDLE WHORLS

In today's western society the spinning of thread and yarn is an activity that very few people even think about. However, for centuries this was an essential and daily activity in many cultures around the world.

Most people today are familiar in theory with the spinning wheel, but less so with the drop spindle, one of the simplest and earliest tools for spinning. A spindle whorl is a weight that is attached to a stick or rod to make a drop spindle. The weight keeps the tension consistent as the fibre - usually wool or cotton - is spun into a thread.

These clay spindle whorls, or "torteros", were made in Ecuador approximately 1,000 years ago. Exact dating would require the partial destruction of at least one whorl, but our research indicates that that they are likely authentic. In a large piece, such as a pot or sculpture, one would be more suspicious of fakes, but for such small pieces the work to reproduce the extensive decoration would not be worth the time and effort. The decoration on the whorls includes pelicans and the jaguar, both creatures important to the people in Central and South America.

ACCESSION NUMBER: 730.00, 1528.00, 1529.00, 1530.00, 1531.00
CRAFTSPERSON: Unknown
DIMENSIONS: 1.8cm (h) x 2cm (dia), 1.6cm x 1.7cm, 0.7cm x 1.5cm, 2.1cm x 0.5cm, 1.5cm x 1.3cm.
MATERIALS: clay
DATE: approx 1000 BP

42. BATTENBURG LACE COLLAR

It is hard to imagine today, but lace making used to be a major industry and it was sometimes a cause of war. In the days before machine-made laces, all lace was made painstakingly by hand, which made it a valuable commodity. Patterns and techniques were guarded from others and lace could easily be identified with a certain district or area in Europe.

Battenburg lace was a successful way of shortening the lace making process. Also called tape lace, it is made by first sewing a thin piece of fabric tape to a printed fabric pattern. The areas between the tapes were then filled in using a needle and thread, again according to a pattern. This is much less time consuming than bobbin lace, which can involve dozens of sets of individual bobbins with threads, or needle lace, where each element is made using only one needle and thread. Battenburg lace was never considered as fine a lace as bobbin lace or needle lace, but it still became very popular in the late 19th century.

This piece was never finished. It is still attached to the fabric pattern and there are areas in the lace that are not filled in accordingly.

ACCESSION NUMBER: 754.00
CRAFTSPERSON: Unknown
DIMENSIONS: 61cm (w) x 101cm (l)
MATERIALS: cotton
DATE: Early 20th Century

43. BOBBIN LACE HANDKERCHIEF

Bobbin lace, likely developed in the 15th or 16th century, is a lace making technique that involves the use of up to a hundred or more bobbins. Each bobbin is wound with a single thread that is tied and woven into lace. While it is being worked, the lace is supported on a pillow that has a paper pattern, called a pricking, laid on top. The pattern is pricked with pins, which provides a structure around which the bobbin threads are tied.

Elise Osted took up bobbin lace after immigrating to Canada from Denmark in the mid 1950s. After her three children were no longer at home, she discovered a passion for fibre arts, and also became an accomplished weaver, teaching both lace making and weaving at the CRAFTS GUILD OF MANITOBA.

This handkerchief has a linen centre with tonder lace, a form of bobbin lace, around the edge. The small heart motif is called the *"Little Heart of Denmark"*. The lace has been attached to the fabric using a distinctive Danish stitch called nonnehulsøm.

ACCESSION NUMBER: 785.00
TITLE: Heart of Denmark
CRAFTSPERSON: Elise Osted
DIMENSIONS: 21.5cm (w) x 21.5cm (l)
MATERIALS: linen, cotton
DATE: Late 20th century

44. SIFTON SPINNING WHEEL

The Sifton spinning wheel is an important part of Manitoba and Canadian crafts history. The small community of Sifton, 30 kilometres north of Dauphin, was the centre of an active wool milling and related manufacturing industry between 1930 and the 1950s.

John Weslowski, a blacksmith, first made these wheels in the early 1930s. He saw that many farmers could not afford to buy woollen garments and he decided to manufacture spinning wheels so that people could make their own warm winter clothing. The wheel was based on one he imported from the Ukraine. The wheels were advertised in the Dauphin Herald, and demand increased quickly. The blacksmith shop soon became the Spin-Well Manufacturing Company, run by John and his brother George. By 1938 they were producing 20 wheels a day. The company also purchased industrial equipment for processing wool, and employed up to 40 people for the manufacture of comforters, parkas, and other woollens. The local railway station agent, Willard McPhedrain, was the main organizer of an expanded company, Spin-Well Woollen Mill. He imported wool from other parts of Canada and promoted the company's products. McPhedrain also founded Mary Maxim Co. Ltd, manufacturing sweaters at first based on designs by Mary Maximchuk of Sifton. The Mary Maxim wool and pattern company thrives today as a mail-order business.

After wool production was moved out of Sifton, the Spin-Well Manufacturing Company was purchased in 1946 by Metro Lozinski, who continued to produce "Spin-Well" wheels and hand and drum carders under the name of Made-Well Manufacturing Co. These items were marketed across Canada. Simpler but functional models of these same items are still produced on demand in the same factory in Sifton by Metro's son, Don Lozinski.

ACCESSION NUMBER: 828.00
CRAFTSPERSON: Spin-Well Manufacturing Co. or Made-Well Manufacturing Co., Sifton, Manitoba, Canada
DIMENSIONS: 49cm (w) x 77cm (h) x 48cm (l)
MATERIALS: wood, metal fittings, cotton string
DATE: 1930s – 1946

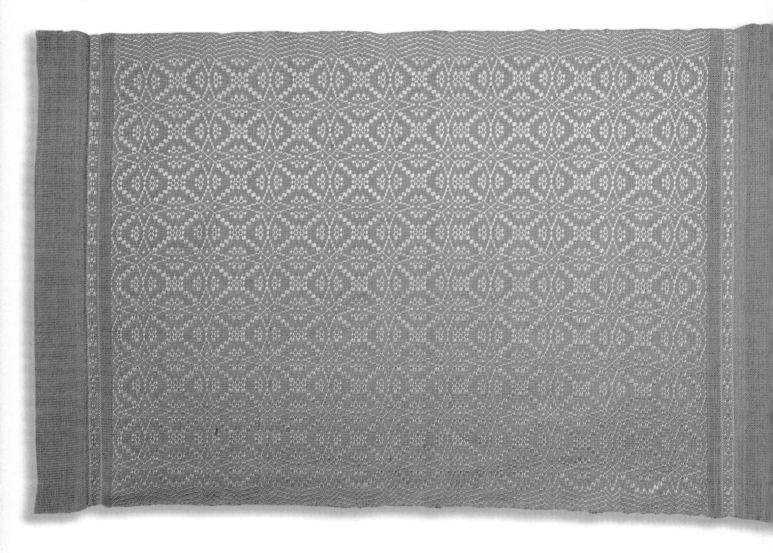

45. WOVEN PLACEMAT

This placemat was woven by Elsie Ogston on a 4-harness loom with natural linen used for the warp and the tabby weft, and rayon for the pattern weft. The threading draft is the Maltese cross, an overshot pattern.

ACCESSION NUMBER: 898.00
CRAFTSPERSON: Elsie Ogston
DIMENSIONS: 32.5cm (w) x 48cm (l)
MATERIALS: natural linen, satin rayon, tabby linen
DATE: c. 1950

46. HARDANGER TRAY CLOTH

Hardanger is one of the best known Norwegian crafts. This tray cloth is a very traditional sample of Norwegian Hardanger, using kloster blocks, woven bars, lace and twisted-cross fillings, fagotting and eyelet to achieve a lace like appearance for an embroidered piece.

Jennie Webb, nee Rudduck, was born in Michigan, but moved with her husband to Winnipeg in 1927. She joined the Crafts Guild of Manitoba in 1944 and quickly became involved in all aspects of the Guild, serving from 1950 to 1952, as Vice-President and on numerous committees. She was also the keeper of the Permanent Collection for about nine years, until 1981 when Ivy Rollo took on the task of managing the growing collection. Jenny Webb was also a charter member of the Canadian Crafts Council. In addition to her support of the Guild, Jennie Webb was a sewer, embroiderer, crocheter, and knitter. In later years she took up weaving, English smocking and Turkish lace.

ACCESSION NUMBER: 902.00
CRAFTSPERSON: Jennie Webb
DIMENSIONS: 26.5cm (w) x 36cm (l)
MATERIALS: open weave cotton/linen with
    white cotton thread
DATE: c. 1950s

47. CARVED DUCK

Don Phalen began carving ducks and other birds in
1985, and thus, he had only been carving for three years
when he made this piece to celebrate the CRAFTS GUILD
OF MANITOBA's 60th anniversary in 1988.

ACCESSION NUMBER: 907.00
CRAFTSPERSON: Donald Phalen
DIMENSIONS: 13.7 cm (w) x 15cm (h) x 28.3cm (l)
MATERIALS: tupelo wood
DATE: 1988

48. DRAWN THREAD RUNNER

A somewhat complex study of traditional drawn-thread work, this runner features four distinctive borders, all of which display particular examples of this technique. Drawn-thread work entails counting and removing horizontal (weft) threads as well as vertical (warp) threads from specific points in the fabric. These areas are then reinforced with particular embroidery techniques. Of special note is the widest border that comprises groups of vertical threads gathered in the centre, numerous woven wheels and needle woven crosses. Spanish openwork, the most difficult technique, fills the corners.

Margaret Wilson, was obviously a highly skilled embroiderer. She was born in 1842, and her ancestors were United Empire Loyalists. Married in 1873, she and her husband had a fruit farm that was located between St. Catharines and Port Delusie, Ontario.

Mrs. Wilson's granddaughter, Margaret Pugh, upon donating this runner to the MANITOBA CRAFTS MUSEUM AND LIBRARY in the 1990s, said that it had been in the family for several generations.

ACCESSION NUMBER: 955.00
CRAFTSPERSON: Margaret Wilson
DIMENSIONS: 43cm (w) x 137.5cm (l)
MATERIALS: evenweave linen, cotton
DATE: Late 19th – Early 20th Century

49. NEEDLE LACE COLLAR

Imagine doing an embroidered piece where there is no backing fabric and all the stitches are looped only to the other stitches in the piece. This is how needle lace is made. It takes an incredibly long time to make a complete piece like this collar. Up to 6,000 buttonhole stitches are required to fill one square inch of space.

ACCESSION NUMBER: 1055.00
CRAFTSPERSON: Unknown
DIMENSIONS: 48cm (w) x 68.5cm (l)
MATERIALS: Linen
DATE: Late 19th – Early 20th Century

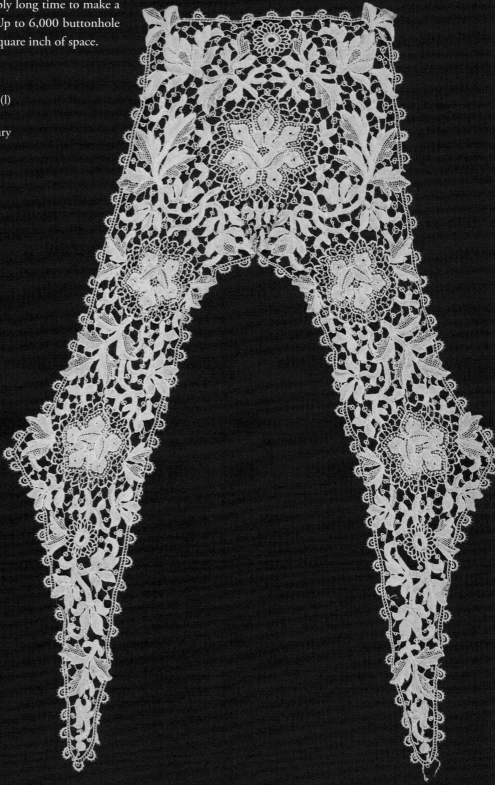

50. EMBROIDERED GAMES TABLE COVER

Little is known about this table cover. However, judging from the images of playing cards, poker chips, racing greyhounds and horses, all of which are beautifully executed in a relatively fine needlepoint count, it might be assumed that the maker was a serious "games" participant. Otherwise, why would so much time be spent on something that was not meaningful to the stitcher? Gaming, as it was frequently called in Victorian times, and well into the 20th century, included numerous card games that involved betting and gambling on horses, dogs and even other animals trained to fight. As card games evolved over time and bridge became a favourite activity for many, it is thought that possibly this family heirloom became known as the "bridge table" cover. In fact, it does fit a folding card table.

This games table cover was fashioned by Sadie Lyons and donated to the Manitoba Crafts Museum and Library in 1990 by her daughter, Enid Lyons.

ACCESSION NUMBER: 1209.00
CRAFTSPERSON: Sadie Lyons
DIMENSIONS: 77.5cm (w) x 84.7cm (l)
MATERIALS: canvas, needlepoint wools, and brown corduroy
DATE: 1920s – 1940s

51. BIRCH BARK BITING

If a craft can become extinct, birch bark biting was recently on the edge. It has been done traditionally by women in many Aboriginal communities in Canada for centuries. The maker uses thin pieces of birch bark to create wonderful designs simply by folding the bark and biting in strategic locations. The key is being able to visualize the end result while the bark is still folded, because the design is only revealed once it is unfolded. The final product is best seen when held up to the light, so that the natural colour of the bark glows and the design is illuminated from the back.

At one point it seemed that only one birch bark biter remained, the famous Angelique Merasty, and she died in 1995. During the 1980s and 1990s a small number of women, including Sally Milne from La Ronge, Saskatchewan decided to learn this ancient technique. Milne is now acknowledged as one of Canada's better birch bark biters and is helping to revive a traditional Aboriginal activity that almost disappeared.

The original purpose of the birch bark biting ranges from a fun activity to occupy cold winter days, to providing patterns for beadwork, embroidery and on birch bark baskets, to providing a spiritual activity for the makers.

ACCESSION NUMBER: 1330.00
CRAFTSPERSON: Sally Milne
DIMENSIONS: 23.5cm (w) x 22.9cm (l)
MATERIALS: birch bark, red felt pen
DATE: 1993

52. BEADED BAG

This beaded chatelaine purse is made from such tiny beads and using such a detailed pattern that MANITOBA CRAFTS MUSEUM AND LIBRARY staff and volunteers initially debated whether it was even hand made. Finally it was concluded that it had indeed been made by hand, using the bead weaving technique.

Bead weaving can be done with or without a loom. The technique involves many warp threads and usually a double weft, where one weft thread is passed under the warp threads and the other is passed above the weft threads, with both going through the holes in the beads.

These purses were popular in the late Victorian period and were usually worn attached to a belt, rather than carried. The word *chatelaine* probably comes from the French "chateau" or castle, and "laine" or wool, and refers to someone who held keys to the linen cupboard in a castle. The word then became attached to any purse used to carry the keys, and then to all small beaded purses like this one.

ACCESSION NUMBER: 1333.00
CRAFTSPERSON: Unknown
DIMENSIONS: 14.9cm (w) x 24.9cm (l)
MATERIALS: glass & metal beads, metal, silk
DATE: c. 1900

53. EMBROIDERED BAG

This little handbag is embroidered in counted thread techniques, including cross stitch, back stitch and satin stitches. The designs appear to be Bulgarian and in fact almost identical images have been found in a DMC design book titled Bulgarian Embroideries.

Donated to the CRAFTS GUILD OF MANITOBA by the DUGALD COSTUME MUSEUM (now called the Costume Museum of Canada) in the 1990s, it originally was part of a travelling exhibition spearheaded by Lady Tweedsmuir, wife of Canada's Governor General in 1937. The Women's Institute of Manitoba, assisted by the

CRAFTS GUILD OF MANITOBA, amassed an assortment of hand made articles that included embroideries, knitting, weaving and rug hooking which became known as the Tweedsmuir Collection.

ACCESSION NUMBER: 1345.00
CRAFTSPERSON: Unknown
DIMENSIONS: 12.8cm (w) x 19.1cm (l)
MATERIALS: evenweave natural linen, embroidery floss, wool, zipper, polished peach pit
DATE: Early 20th Century

54. GUATEMALAN DROP SPINDLE

This piece was purchased by Gillian Bird at a market in Guatemala in the mid 1990s. Made from a sharpened and fire-hardened piece of wood with a ceramic bead for a spindle whorl, this tool could be easily made by people in the region. Although the weaving tradition has been diminishing in recent years, many Guatemalans and other Central and South Americans still produce their own spun cotton and wool. These threads and yarns are woven, often on a backstrap loom, to make wonderful clothing and rugs.

ACCESSION NUMBER: 1403.00
CRAFTSPERSON: Unknown
DIMENSIONS: 41.5cm (l) x 3cm (dia)
MATERIALS: wood, ceramic bead, cotton
DATE: c. 1992

55. VASE

Using a zinc-based glaze and specific kiln temperatures, Nonie Chalmers can make crystals form in the glaze. This technique, used by only a small number of potters in the world, creates a frost-like pattern on the surface of the pot.

ACCESSION NUMBER: 1424.00
CRAFTSPERSON: Nonie Chalmers
DIMENSIONS: 24.5cm (h) x 13cm (dia)
MATERIALS: clay, zinc based glaze
DATE: c. 1994

56. ICELANDIC KNITTED SCARF

Many marriage traditions have been reflected in hand crafted items. These fine knitted shawls were often made to be part of a wedding outfit. The belief is that the shawl should be knitted finely enough to be able to pass through the wedding band, representing the lightness of any future worries. The shawl was often given to the first child of the marriage to be used as a blanket.

ACCESSION NUMBER: 1469.00
CRAFTSPERSON: Unknown
DIMENSIONS: 53cm (w) x 103cm (l)
MATERIALS: single thread Icelandic wool
 from the Lopi sheep
DATE: Early 20th Century

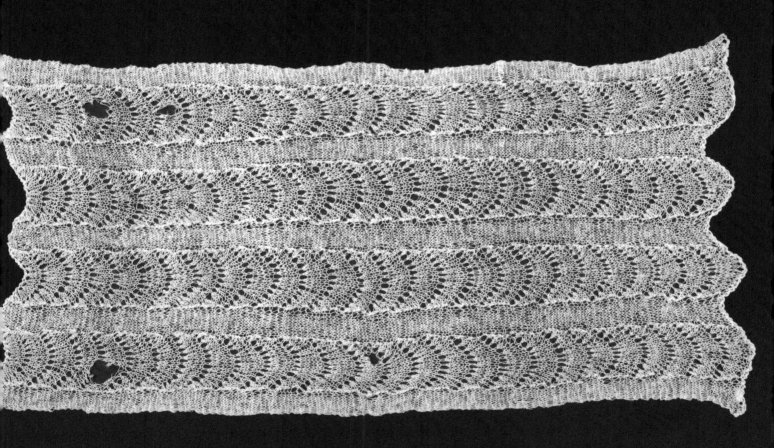

57. RUG HOOKED HANDBAG

When the Manitoba Branch of the Canadian Handicraft Guild was established, one of the goals of the group was to assist women in the rural areas with family life and economics. To that end, they were quick to get involved with an effort by the Women's Institutes to create craft collections that were to be loaned to rural communities to help women with learning practical skills, selling their work to help the family budget, and making good use of the resources available in the community.

This purse was one piece that illustrates how rug hooking can be used to make items other than rugs. It is also making use of hand spun and hand dyed wool, rather than the more traditionally used strips of fabric.

ACCESSION NUMBER: 1503.00
CRAFTSPERSON: Agnes McTaggart
DIMENSIONS: 29.5cm (w) x 25cm (h)
MATERIALS: wool, canvas or burlap, fabric
DATE: c. 1945

58. BOOK PLATE STAMP

In 1948, Gladys Chown, President of the CRAFTS GUILD OF MANITOBA, died quite suddenly while in office. As a permanent memorial to her, the members established a the Gladys Chown Memorial Fund, with proceeds to support THE LIBRARY. Members also decided to name the library in her honour. This bookplate, used to make labels with the GLADYS CHOWN MEMORIAL LIBRARY name, was designed by Eric Bergman, a Manitoba printmaker and a strong supporter of the GUILD.

ACCESSION NUMBER: 1562.00
CRAFTSPERSON: Eric Bergman
DIMENSIONS: 10.4cm (w) x 2.9cm (h) x 7.8cm (l)
MATERIALS: wood, metal
DATE: 1948 – 1949

59. WALL HANGING

This wall hanging is unusual in that Kathleen Baleja, Judy Morningstar and Elaine Rounds all worked independently, and yet the final result was one piece. The three women worked "round robin style" with Elaine Rounds weaving the fabric first. It was then sent by mail to Judy Morningstar who completed the quilted section. Finally, Kathleen Baleja added the stained glass portion. Each part was completed without any input from those who had previously worked on the piece. The three women completed over 50 collaborative pieces in this way.

ACCESSION NUMBER: 1792.00
TITLE: Bronze Landscapes
CRAFTSPERSON: Kathleen Baleja, Judy Morningstar and Elaine Rounds
DIMENSIONS: 62cm (w) x 44cm (l)
MATERIALS: hand woven cloth, cotton, quilt batting, glass, lead
DATE: 1994 – 1995

60. WOOD RELIEF PLAQUE

Guenter Bark learned his craft as a boy in Danzig (now Gdansk), Poland by using his father's tools. Always a lover of nature, he usually depicted wildlife in these detailed reliefs carved from one piece of hardwood.

ACCESSION NUMBER: 1856.00
CRAFTSPERSON: Guenter Bark
DIMENSIONS: 27cm (w) x 64cm (l)
MATERIALS: maple
DATE: Late 20th Century

61. CLAY MOULD

It wasn't until 1979, over 50 years after being established in 1928, that the CRAFTS GUILD OF MANITOBA held its first juried show. As was the practice, GUILD members made customized prize ribbons and awards for participants in these shows. This badge and the mould used to make it were designed and made by Chris Grossman.

ACCESSION NUMBER: 1860.00
CRAFTSPERSON: Chris Grossman
DIMENSIONS: 5cm (h) x 16cm (dia)
MATERIALS: clay, glaze
DATE: 1979

62. GLASS PERFUME BOTTLE

In 1999 the volunteers at the MANITOBA CRAFTS MUSEUM AND LIBRARY visited the studio of Ione Thorkelsson in Roseile, Manitoba. This was part of the annual volunteer appreciation event to recognize the nearly 2,000 hours of work contributed by the 30-40 volunteers. During the visit, Ione demonstrated how she works with the glass in her furnace, and showed the variety of finished products that she sells. At the end of the visit the group purchased this perfume bottle for the museum collection. It was dedicated to Margaret Gaunt, curator of the museum collection from the early 1990s until 1998, who had passed away earlier that year.

ACCESSION NUMBER: 1927.00 & 1927.01
CRAFTSPERSON: Ione Thorkelsson
DIMENSIONS: 11cm (h) x 8.1cm (dia)
MATERIALS: glass
DATE: 1999

63. WOODEN BOX

David and Penny Square are a husband and wife team who have worked together to create small boxes and other wooden containers. This box, like most they have made, depicts an element of Manitoba wildlife. In this case it is a fawn, still with white spots, reflecting their love of living in rural Manitoba. The image on the top is drawn in ink.

ACCESSION NUMBER: 1932.00
CRAFTSPERSON: David and Penny Square
DIMENSIONS: 10cm (w) x 4.7cm (h) x 6.6cm (l)
MATERIALS: satinwood, black walnut, ink,
    metal hinge, varnish
DATE: 1984

64. IRISH CROCHET LACE CHILD'S DRESS

This exquisite child's white dress, carefully crafted in Irish crochet, may have been fashioned for a special event or intended to be a little girl's best Sunday dress, but whatever occasion prompted its creation, it was never worn. The unfinished back closure attests to the fact that when this little gown was nearing completion, for some reason it was packed away out of sight for decades. A beautiful example of Irish crochet with three-dimensional flowers resting on an open mesh, the little dress is completely lined in white silk. It is simply styled with short sleeves and a rounded neckline, both of which are embellished with tiny crocheted scallops, and a high waistline that features crocheted openings, permitting a pink ribbon to softly gather excess fabric.

Taught to children in convents by the nuns as early as 1760, Irish crochet became known in various areas and by the mid 1800s, with the potato famine at its peak, many lay women organized centres and schools where crochet was both taught and sold. While Irish crochet had its beginnings in Paris, France, a unique Irish crochet lace evolved over time. Irish crochet fashions were eventually exported to various countries where local craftspeople also mastered the technique.

ACCESSION NUMBER: 1985.00
CRAFTSPERSON: Unknown
DIMENSIONS: 52cm (w) x 56cm (l)
MATERIALS: white cotton/silk thread, silk lining,
   pastel pink silk ribbon
DATE: Early 1900s

65. FILET CROCHET DOILY

The word "doily" is believed to have originated from an 18th century merchant who sold small pieces of fabric to place under bowls or cups to keep them from marking the table. His name was Mr. D'Oyley. Whether this story is true or not, doilies are a symbol of "old-fashioned" décor.

However, one must not forget the incredible work that has gone into creating these doilies. They were knitted, embroidered, made using bobbin lace, needle lace or tatting techniques, or crocheted. This particular example was made using a filet crochet technique to create the border, and drawn thread with needle weaving to make the centre square.

Many hours would have gone into making pieces such as this, and today they are often dismissed as old and dusty relics from the past.

ACCESSION NUMBER: 1992.00
CRAFTSPERSON: Unknown
DIMENSIONS: 15.5cm (w) x 15.6cm (l)
MATERIALS: cotton
DATE: Late 19th Century

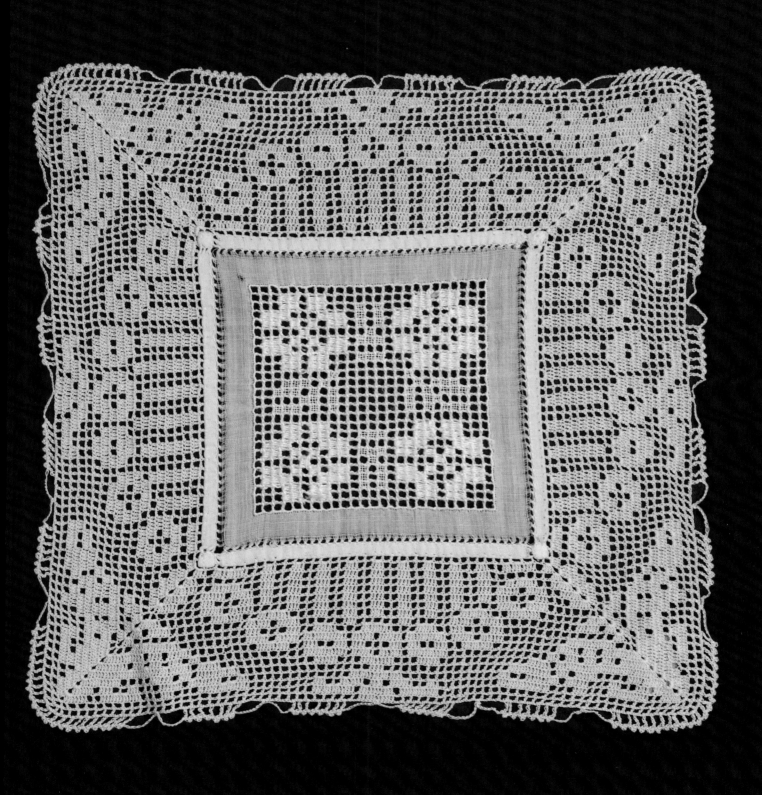

66. RETICELLA MAT

Called *Reticella*, this Italian based technique is a form of needle lace. This piece is small, and was likely planned to be the centre for a tablecloth or perhaps even just a sample of the technique involved. Acknowledged by authorities as on the borderline between embroidery and lace, reticella is an early cutwork technique probably first created as early as the 15th century that continued to evolve into the 17th century. It is mostly associated with the work coming out of Venice during this period.

Depending on the level of work, several threads, or many, are drawn out of fabric and the remaining spaces are filled with needle lace stitches, all of which are based on the buttonhole. This exquisite work was undoubtedly created by a master stitcher, who would have drawn out the maximum number of horizontal and vertical threads, leaving a scant skeleton of fabric. The remaining "ground" on which the stitcher begins working is a very rigid grid. Accordingly, whether less complicated, or as intricate as this work, reticella is relatively easy to identify, as the designs, based on the remaining threads in the fabric, are predominately geometric with numerous decorative squares.

ACCESSION NUMBER: 1993.00
CRAFTSPERSON: Unknown
DIMENSIONS: 17cm (w) x 17cm (l)
MATERIALS: cotton
DATE: 19th Century

67. CLAY BOWL

This bowl is made by Duane Perkins who is known for ceramic pieces that are fairly simple in form, but which have complex designs created by using a variety of glazing techniques.

ACCESSION NUMBER: 2022.00
CRAFTSPERSON: Duane Perkins
DIMENSIONS: 5.4cm (h) x 33.7cm (dia)
MATERIALS: porcelain, copper reduction glaze
DATE: Late 20th Century

68. RUG HOOKED PICTURE

Delza Longman is one of those rare individuals who can make truly beautiful things from discarded material. For many years she has been using only nylons and girls' tights to make hooked pictures, many inspired by the prairies and the natural world. With an interest in the rare and endangered, she often depicts animals, birds and plants that are on the endangered species list, but also does historical subjects such as grain elevators. The colours in the works are all original to the nylons, which often create a challenge due to the changing palate of colours available as the styles come and go over time. She considers it a good day when she receives a bag of old nylons from someone cleaning out a closet. Other sources for nylons include bargain basement sales and factory clearouts.

Her work is done in the style of the Grenfell mission, rather than the coarser wool or fabric strip method favoured by most rug hookers. This finer background cloth and thinner strips of nylons result in a much more detailed image. However, she has been known to pull out and redo large sections of her work when not satisfied with the result.

ACCESSION NUMBER: 2032.02
TITLE: *The Pool*
CRAFTSPERSON: Delza Longman
DIMENSIONS: 20.5cm (w) x 25cm (h)
MATERIALS: nylon stocking, monk's cloth
DATE: 1998

69. WHEAT EMBROIDERY MAT

In 1931, in the early years of the Great Depression, the CRAFTS GUILD OF MANITOBA decision makers agreed that the best way to stimulate continued interest in their endeavours was to feature their very own Manitoba designs on textiles.

Records indicate "there was great delight" when the first wheat design and subsequent embroidery was produced, seemingly by Frances Lount. Other stitchers of the wheat embroideries during more than 65 years of GUILD activity included Ann Dowton, Val Oakley, her sister Clementine, and Susanne Sulkers. Eric Bergman, the well known artist was invited at least twice to update the much admired wheat stalks. The CRAFTS GUILD OF MANITOBA always purchased quality linen from abroad and various members, called "cutters", were responsible for cutting the cloth into the right sizes for placemats, bun warmers and tray cloths.

As was originally stipulated, the wheat embroideries, even as they evolved over the years embellishing both placemats and bun tray cloths, remained the GUILD's ultimate example of their very high handcraft standards.

Heads of State throughout the world, including Queen Elizabeth II, have received these embroideries that were internationally renowned for excellence in both design and execution.

ACCESSION NUMBER: 2036.00
CRAFTSPERSON: Val Oakley
DIMENSIONS: 31.6cm (w) x 44.0cm (l)
MATERIALS: evenweave linen (40 threads to the inch),
   cotton thread
DATE: 1970s

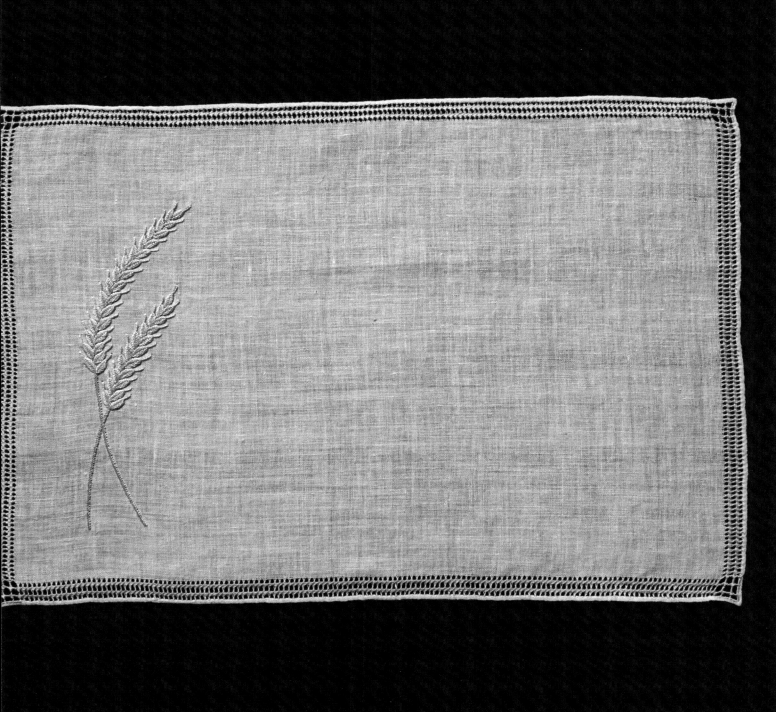

70. SNOW BABY DOLL

Manitoba artisan Jean McMurray conceived the idea for her line of dolls in the early 1960s when she was a young mother up all night with a baby. Dressed in typical Manitoba winter wear, this doll's scarf is knitted and her jacket was inspired by a Hudson's Bay blanket with its bold stripes. The body was fashioned from wire wrapped in wool and glued to a platform of cork. The doll's face is made of fabric, painted and stitched, and the skate blade is made of a paper clip. Jean is well known for her creativity, and she has also taught a variety of workshops in the Winnipeg area.

ACCESSION NUMBER: 2063.00
CRAFTSPERSON: Jean McMurray
DIMENSIONS: 6cm (w) x 10cm (h)
MATERIALS: wool, metal, cork
DATE: 1990s

71. SPIRIT BOWL

As all prairie kids know, potholes in the road that are filled with water get a thin film of ice on them during the first frosty nights in the fall. This bowl is inspired by the form of the hole in the ground with ice covering all or part of the top. Inset into the ice, and mirrored on the bowl, are often leaves and other plant matter that blow around the prairie in the fall.

This piece was acquired during a visit to Barbara Balfour's studio in Stonewall, Manitoba, during a visit by the volunteers of the MANITOBA CRAFTS MUSEUM AND LIBRARY.

ACCESSION NUMBER: 2071.00
TITLE: Spirit Bowl
CRAFTSPERSON: Barbara Balfour
DIMENSIONS: 2.5cm (h) x 22cm (dia)
MATERIALS: clay
DATE: 2003

72. FINGER WEAVING SAMPLE

In 1981 Carol James met a certain Québecois who introduced her to fingerweaving and it was love at first sight. They married in 1985 and moved to Winnipeg in 1990. She soon found herself demonstrating fingerweaving for the Festival du Voyageur and Folklorama. The responsibility of accurate representation of local heritage led her to research historic sashes.

Fingerweaving is a "low tech" method for producing cloth. The hands are the only tools needed. This is the technique used to create the traditional sash of the Voyageurs. Because of the arrow pattern which occurs in the centre of these belts, they are called "Arrow Sashes" or in French, "Ceinture Fléchées".

All threads are lengthwise (called the warp) in the fabric and each thread takes a turn at being the width-wise thread (known as the weft). This movement also causes a tangled mass called the false weave that the weaver must periodically untangle as the sash progresses.

Hearsay has it that upon arriving in the Red River Settlement Bishop Provencher wrote to his superiors in Montreal saying, "Send me a dozen of those Assomption belts. The people here are crazy about them". Paintings of the period indicated that the sashes were indeed very popular items. Jean-Baptiste Lagimodière and his grandson Louis Riel wore them. The St. Boniface Museum holds a sash worn by Elzéar Goulet and the Manitoba Museum collection features sashes belonging to George Simpson McTavish and Lord Strathcona.

It was in the context of research that Carol first contacted the MANITOBA CRAFTS MUSEUM AND LIBRARY, only to discover to her dismay a serious gap in the collection. This sample represents her effort to rectify that situation.

ACCESSION NUMBER: 2150.02
CRAFTSPERSON: Carol James
DIMENSIONS: 15cm (w) x 30cm (l)
MATERIALS: wool
DATE: 2004

73. KNITTED SWEATER

This sweater was one of Carol McCann's first knitted pieces. An experienced doll maker and embroiderer, Carol started knitting in the early 1980s. Within a few years she was making one-of-a-kind pieces for sale in boutiques in the Toronto area.

ACCESSION NUMBER: 2159.02

CRAFTSPERSON: Carol McCann

DIMENSIONS: 40cm (w) x 60cm (l)

MATERIALS: wool, synthetic fibres, metallic thread, chenille, wood buttons

DATE: 1982

74. LIQUID CLAY POT

Ken Chernavitch is known for using a substance called liquid clay to create most of his pieces, including this square pot. To complete a piece, Chernavitch starts with a plaster base, onto which he squeezes out a quantity of clay required for the final size of the piece. He then adds any colours in the same liquid clay format. The plaster absorbs most of the water making the material like soft leather. At this point, he can assemble the sides (as in this piece) or mould the slab into a cylinder or other shape.

ACCESSION NUMBER: 2171.00
CRAFTSPERSON: Ken Chernavitch
DIMENSIONS: 17.7cm (w) x 19.2cm (h) x 18.1cm (l)
MATERIALS: clay
DATE: 1980

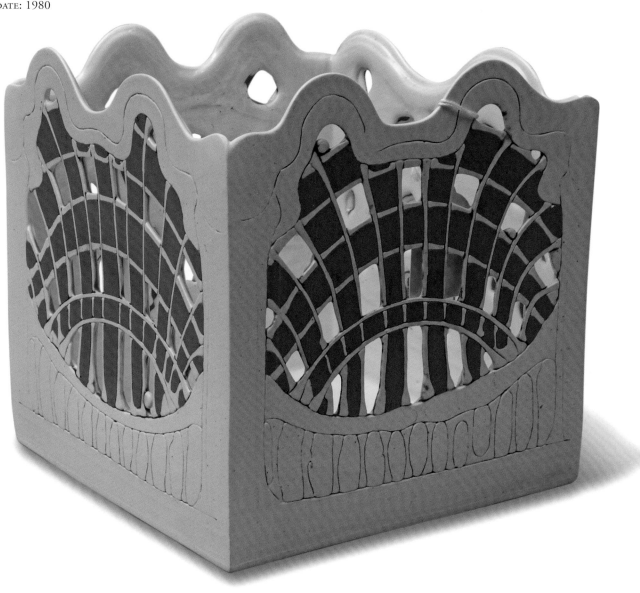

75. CORN DOLLIE

As a prairie province, Manitoba has always recognized agriculture as a vital component of our landscape, culture, economy and identity. This artifact has its roots in the celebration of harvest –the events, superstitions, and traditions – that has been so important to people for generations.

Corn dollies are thought to have originated as a way of saving the last piece of the harvest for the year to ensuring success the following year. The term "corn" is used in Britain as a general term for all grains and the word "dollie" is a corruption of the word "idol".

This particular piece is sometimes known as the "Corn Goddess" or the "Swedish Oat Queen".

ACCESSION NUMBER: 2174.00
CRAFTSPERSON: Pat Watson
DIMENSIONS: 30cm (w) x 45cm (h) x 16cm (d)
MATERIALS: wheat, green ribbon
DATE: 1990s

ARTISTS

GROUP PROJECTS

Members of the Macramé Group
of the Craft Guild of Manitoba
for piece ....#34
Anderson, Rheba
Brewster, Rose
Brown, Louise
Carstens, Mary
Grant, Margaret
Knudson, Margaret
Lawrence, Selina (Convenor)
Manson, Gladys
Melville, Eleanor
Mitchell, Margaret
Mullin, Henrietta
Profit, Margaret
Rochelle, Elsie
Shuttleworth, Charlotte
Strong, Gerdine Crawford
Tyderkie, Shirley

Members of the Embroidery Group
of the Crafts Guild of Manitoba
for piece ....#12
Ashmore, R.
Atha, V.R.
Ayre, Veran
Cunningham, Helen
Dowton, Anne
Gillespie, R. Hilda
Green, E.

Harvey, V.
Heise, Phoebe E.
Horne, J.
Hugill, Lyla G.
Lawrence, Selina
Lowe, A
MacLeod, Mary
Marshall, Flora
McHugh, Laura
McLaren, A.R.
Newman, M
Osborne, Sophia May (designer)
Phair, M.L.
Radford, K.M. Fayden
Robinson, E.
Sawyer, P.
Scrimshaw, E.H.
Skelton, J.
Stone, M.J.
Webb, Jennie B.
Whitelaw, Catharine
Whitworth, M.A.
Wilson, R.
Young, E.
Young, M.A.

Members of the Embroidery Group
of the Crafts Guild of Manitoba for
piece ....#6
Dale, Mitzi Anderson
Howorth, F.
Hugill, W.M.
Hutzulak, P.
Istvanffy, Zola
Juettner, G.D.
Larrson, W.
Whitworth, M.
Wilson, H.
Young, F.

SELECTED BIBLIOGRAPHY FOR 75TH ANNIVERSARY BOOK

Bryson, Agnes F. *Ayrshire Needlework*. London: B. T. Batsford Ltd., 1989.

Buxton-Keenlyside, Judith. *Selected Canadian Spinning Wheels in Perspective: An Analytical Approach*. Ottawa: National Museums of Canada, 1980.

Collier, Ann. *The Art of Lacemaking*. London: Bracken Books, 1986.

Crawford, Gail. *Studio Ceramics in Canada*. Fredericton: Goose Lane Editions, 2005.

Crandall, Richard C. *Inuit Art: A history*. London: McFarland & Company, Inc., Publishers, 2000.

D'Arcy, Eithne. *Irish Crochet Lace*. Mountrath: The Dolmen Press Ltd., 1984.

Dabbs, Christine. *Crazy Quilting*. Nashville: Rutledge Hill Press, 1998.

Dumont, Katie. *The New Macramé: Contemporary Knotted Jewellery and Accessories*. New York: Lark Books, 2000.

Engelstad, Helen. *Native Art of Norway*. New York: Frederick A. Praeger Publishers, 1967.

Finseth, Claudia Rüf. "The Scandinavian Tradition of Narrative Textiles", *Scandinavian Folk Patterns for Counted Thread Embroidery*. Seattle: 1987.

From, Dot. *The History of the Crafts Guild of Manitoba*. Dot From: Winnipeg, 2001.

Gostelow, Mary. *Embroidery: Traditional designs, techniques and patterns from around the world*. London: Marshall Cavendish Editions, 1997.

Green, H. Gordon, Editor. *A Heritage of Canadian Handicrafts*. Toronto: McClelland and Stewart Limited, 1967.

Haertig, Evelyn. *Antique Combs and Purses*. Santa Ana: Gallery Graphics Press, 1983.

Hail, Barbara A. and Kate C. Duncan. *Out of the North: Subarctic Collection of the Haffenreffer Museum of Anthropology*. Bristol: The Haffenreffer Museum of Anthropology, 1989.

Hail, Barbara A. *Hau, Kóla: The Plains Indian Collection of the Haffenreffer Museum of Anthropology*. Bristol: Haffenreffer Museum of Anthropology, 1980.

Holm, Bill. *Spirit and Ancestor: A century of northwest coast Indian art at the Burke Museum*. Toronto: Douglas & McIntyre, 1987.

Jackson, Emily. *Old Handmade Lace: With a dictionary of lace*. New York: Dover Publications, Inc., 1861.

Jarry, Madeleine. *World Tapestry: From its Origins to the Present*. New York: G. P. Putnam's Sons, 1968.

Jones, Laura. *Ireland's Traditional Crafts Ed. David Shaw-Smith*. London: Thames and Hudson, 1984.

Jones, Rebecca. *The Complete Book of Tatting: Everything you wanted to know but couldn't find out about Shuttle Lace*. Berkley: Lacis, 1985.

Keller, Doxie and Lois MacNeil. *Country Straw 1*. Hutchinson: Wheat Weaving, Inc., 1981.

King, Donald. *Samplers*. London: Her Majesty's Stationary Office, 1960.

Kliot, Jules. *Tatting: Designs from Victorian Lace Craft*. Berkley: Lacis Publishing, 1978.

Konior, Mary. *Heritage Crochet: An Analysis*. London: Dryad Press, Ltd., 1987.

Lambeth, M. *A Golden Dolly: The art, mystery and history of corn dollies*. London: John Baker (Publishers), 1969.

Laverty, Paula. *Silk Stocking Mats: Hooked Mats of the Grenfell Mission*. London: McGill-Queen's University Press, 2005.

Lind, Vibeke. *Knitting in the Nordic Tradition*. Ashville: Lark Books, 1984.

SELECTED BIBLIOGRAPHY
FOR 75TH ANNIVERSARY BOOK

Maidens, Ena. *The Technique of Irish Crochet Lace.* London: B.J. Batsford Ltd., 1986.

Majka, Christopher and Sheilagh Hunt. *Polish Folk Costumes.* Halifax: Empty Mirrors Press, 1991.

Manitoba Crafts Museum and Library. *Accessions Book.* Winnipeg, Manitoba. 2006.

Montupet, Janine and Ghislaine Schoeller. *Lace: The elegant web.* New York: Harry N. Abrams, Inc., 1988.

Morrison, David and Georges-Hébert Germain. *Inuit: Glimpses of an arctic Past.*
   Hull: Canadian Museum of Civilization, 1995.

Oaks, Jill and Rick Rieve. *Our Boots: An Inuit women's art.* Toronto: Douglas & McIntyre, 1995.

Pagold, Susanne. *Nordic Knitting: Thirty-one Patterns in the Scandinavian Tradition.*
   Loveland: Interweave Press, 1987.

Philbrook Museum of Art. *Woven Worlds: Basketry from the Clarke Field Collection.*
   Tulsa: The Philbrook Museum of Art, 2001.

Plath, Iona. *The Decorative Arts of Sweden.* New York: Dover Publications Inc., 1948.

Pu, Lu. *Designs of Chinese Indigo Batik.* New York and Beijing: Lee Publishers Group, Inc.,
   and New World Press, 1981.

Rivers, Victoria Z. *The Shining Cloth: Dress and adornment that glitters.* New York: Thames & Hudson, Inc., 1999.

Rounds, Elaine. "Elaine Rounds: Manitoba Designer Craftsperson", *A Weaver's Dozen.*

Rutt, Richard. *A History of Hand Knitting.* Loveland: Interweave Press, 1987.

Sandberg, Gösta. *Indigo Textiles: Technique and History.* London: A & C Black, 1989.

Scott, Shirley A. *Canada Knits: Craft and Comfort in a Northern Land.* Toronto: McGraw-Hill Ryerson, 1990.

Square, David Shath. *The Veneering Book.* Newtown: Taunton Press, 1995.

Stearns, Marilyn. *The Art of Grain Weaving.* North Springfield: Red House Press, 1981.

Stewart, Hilary. *Cedar: Tree of Life to the Northwest Coast Indians.* Toronto: Douglas & McIntyre, 1984.

Thompson, Judy. *From the Land: Two Hundred Years of Dene Clothing.*
   Hull: Canadian Musuem of Civilization, 1994.

Thorkelsson, Ione. "Ione Thorkelsson: Glassblower – Carman, Manitoba", *The Craftsman's Way: Canadian Expressions Ed. John Flanders.* Toronto: University of Toronto Press, 1981, 87-9.

Tsang, Ka Bo. *Touched by Indigo: Chinese Blue-and-White Textiles and Embroidery.*
   Toronto: Royal Ontario Museum, 2005.

Tyrchniewicz, Peggy. *Ethnic Folk Costumes in Canada.* Winnipeg: Hyperion Press Limited, 1979.

Unknown. "David and Penny Square", *The Manitoba Collection: The Catalogue.* (1987- 88).

Waterman, Martha. *Traditional Knitted Lace Shawls.* Loveland: Interweave Press, 1998.

White, Emmie. *Corn Dollies from the start.* London: G. Bell & Sons Ltd., 1978.

Wilcox, Claire. "Bags, Purses and Châtelaines: 1830-1880", *Bags.* London: V & A Publications, 1999.

Wilson, Erica. "Introduction", *Crewel Embroidery.* New York: Charles Scribner's Sons, 1962, 10-27.

Winnipeg Art Gallery. *Manitoba Quilts and Ceramics: A survey of contemporary quilting and pottery in Southern and Central Manitoba.* Winnipeg: The Bulman Brothers, 1971.

THE MANITOBA CRAFTS MUSEUM AND LIBRARY

MANITOBA CRAFTS MUSEUM AND LIBRARY is a repository of a wealth of information and expertise on the practice and preservation of all forms of craft. Through its artifact and book collection, exhibitions, public programs and educational outreach, MCML increases community appreciation of the unique artistic and social role of craft in current and traditional society.

With over 5,000 artifacts in its collection, the MUSEUM is a legacy of traditional handicrafts and tools originating primarily from Manitoba. In addition to the material history of MCML's parent body, the CRAFTS GUILD OF MANITOBA, the collection represents the rich history of Manitoba crafts artists and the variety of craft traditions brought to Canada by immigrants from around the world.

The Library holds over 2,500 contemporary and historical books and hundreds of magazines, scrapbooks and craft patterns. It is a unique resource for the craft artist, historian, and teacher. It is a lending library for MCML members, but all visitors can use the library on site.

With their exclusive focus on traditional and contemporary handcrafts, the Museum and Library collections together form the only organization of its kind in Canada.

MANITOBA CRAFTS MUSEUM AND LIBRARY
1B-183 Kennedy Street
Winnipeg, Manitoba
R3C 1S6

(204) 487-6117 ph. & fax.
mcml1@mts.net
www.mts.net/~mcml